CHURCHILL'S
WAR IN WORDS

HIS FINEST QUOTES, 1939–1945

Jonathan Asbury

Published by IWM, Lambeth Road, London SE1 6HZ
© The Trustees of the Imperial War Museum, 2017.
This edition printed 2018.

ISBN 978-1-904897-36-1

A catalogue record for this book is available from the British Library.
Printed and bound in Italy by Printer Trento
Colour reproduction by DL Imaging

Every effort has been made to contact all copyright holders.
The publishers will be glad to make good in future editions any
error or omission brought to their attention.

10 9 8 7 6 5 4 3 2

Front cover image: (composite), © IWM HU 90343 (detail, this image
has been artificially coloured), © IWM HU 87413 (detail)
Back cover image: © IWM NYP 68075

MIX
Paper from
responsible sources
FSC® C015829

CONTENTS

INTRODUCTION

Winston Churchill once described words as 'the only things that last for ever'. He was talking in particular about historical quotations, which he believed offered the reader a direct, unexpurgated link to the past. They are not 'mere relics' he explained; they possess a 'pristine vital force'. The idea of this book is to harness that force to illuminate our understanding of Churchill and his role in the Second World War.

There have, of course, been countless millions of words written on this subject since the war ended – not least by Churchill himself – but not a single one of them appears in this book. We have chosen instead to include only those words written or spoken in the momentous six-year period from 1939 through to 1945. This is Churchill's war as it appeared at the time, when the twin prospects of defeat and victory lay shrouded in a fog of decisions yet to be made, risks yet to be taken and battles yet to be fought. They are words freighted with fear, anxiety, disappointment, anger, relief, hope and elation – words that avoid the editorialising and revisionism of memoir and history to take you directly to the messy realities of the 'there and then'.

The majority of the quotations are taken from Churchill himself: from the speeches he delivered in the House of Commons, over the airwaves or during his travels; from the many minutes and memoranda he produced to influence the course of the war; and from the often revealing remarks he made in private conversation with friends and colleagues. However, we have also included quotations *about* Churchill as well as by him, again drawing only on diaries and letters written at the time. Family and friends, allies and enemies, politicians and civil servants, military leaders and diplomats, members of the armed services and of the public –

we will hear from them all. That way, we can see how Churchill was viewed at the time – in public and in private, both by his supporters and his critics.

We have chosen to present the material in chronological rather than thematic order. Each chapter covers a calendar year so that as you delve further into the book a story emerges – month by month, week by week, and even day by day – that we hope says much about the evolution of the war and Churchill's role in it. At the beginning of each chapter you will also find a brief summary of the year in question, putting the selected quotations into their historical context.

That then is one way in which this book explores *Churchill's War in Words*. But it also does so on a completely different level. American war correspondent Edward R. Murrow famously said that Churchill 'mobilised the English language and sent it into battle'. In this book we can see some of that process in action. We can get a sense of the changing tone, content and frequency of his speeches; discover how he courted allies or consciously tried to shape the public mood; and see how often

he had to employ the power of his rhetoric to carry the day – or save his skin – in Parliament or Cabinet. Most fascinatingly of all, we can see how these speeches were received. How did those famous phrases – the fighting on the beaches, the finest hours and the many and the few – go down at the time? Did they hit home immediately and with everyone? How did they help shape perceptions of Churchill? And what effect, if any, did they have on the course of the war?

Through the quotes given about Churchill, we can also trace another story that helps illuminate the strange complexity of his personality and career. Modern readers tend to think of Churchill in shorthand terms as 'the greatest Briton' or the man who masterminded the country's victory in the Second World War. This can be hard to reconcile with his prolonged period in the political wilderness before the war, and his abrupt departure from office before the conflict had even ended. This book aims to shed light on these apparent contradictions. It explores how Churchill was viewed by others during this period; it shows how his words and behaviour contributed to these perceptions; it brings out the role played by factors such as party politics, travel and illness; and it reveals how the man himself viewed the oscillations in his popularity. By adding a wealth of nuance and colour, it carves out the man from the myth, and presents a story all the more remarkable for it.

No book of this kind could ever hope to be comprehensive; it barely makes a dent in the gargantuan amount of material written and spoken by and about Churchill during the Second World War. In fact it represents only a fraction of the quotations gathered together in the course of compiling this book. In making a final selection, we have tried to take a number of factors into account. We have naturally been on the look-out for memorable, witty or well-crafted turns of phrase, but others have been included for the insights that they offer, the events they refer to, or the telling scenes they depict. Some quotations are lengthy extracts from important speeches; others are as short as a couple of words – often in reaction to those same speeches. We have tried to draw on a wide variety of sources but we have also returned to some at frequent intervals in order to convey the evolving nature of the story. Finally, and most importantly, the vast bulk of the quotations come from Winston Churchill himself. On the one hand, this is his story; and on the other, he tells it so wonderfully well.

Previous Page
Churchill en route to the House of Commons, August 1944.

'THE ONLY ENGLISHMAN HITLER IS AFRAID OF'

After his warnings about Nazi Germany are proved correct, Churchill returns to high office on a wave of public popularity but to a mixed reception in the corridors of Whitehall.

By January 1939, Churchill had been out of government office for almost a decade. For much of that time he had criticised the foreign and defence policies of successive governments and prime ministers, issuing repeated warnings about the growing military threat of Nazi Germany. His was the proverbial 'voice crying in the wilderness' and it had never cried more stridently than during the Munich Crisis of September the previous year, when Hitler had threatened to annexe part of Czechoslovakia. According to Churchill, Britain had faced a choice between 'war and shame' and the government, by making concessions to Germany, had chosen shame. They were strong words – not easily forgotten or forgiven by those who believed in Prime Minister

Neville Chamberlain's commitment to conciliation and negotiation as a means of securing peace.

One thing that both sides could agree on after Munich was that the government's policy towards Germany would have to change if Hitler's aggression continued. As events unfolded – and particularly when German troops marched into the rest of Czechoslovakia in March 1939 – the gap between government policy and Churchill's own position began to close. Consequently, as spring became summer, and the shadow of military confrontation loomed larger, there came repeated calls in the press for his restoration to the Cabinet.

These calls were fuelled in part by the powerful speeches that Churchill continued to make both inside and outside the House of Commons. His trenchant views and resonant phrasing made for a potent mix, no longer dismissed as 'alarmist' or 'war-mongering', but chiming in with the mood of the public.

Although Churchill was not without his supporters in Parliament, there were many politicians and civil servants who viewed his growing popularity with dismay. His views on the menace of Hitler may have been vindicated, but for his critics there remained many question marks over his judgment and temperament. Many were unable to forget Churchill's role in the First World War when, as First Lord of the Admiralty (the political head of the Royal Navy), he had masterminded the ambitious but ultimately disastrous Dardanelles Campaign. Designed to knock Turkey out of the war, it had ended instead with a humiliating withdrawal of Allied troops from a costly and bloody campaign, and had earlier led to Churchill's unceremonious departure from office. The episode reinforced his growing reputation for recklessness – a characterisation that would prove hard

to shake. On the other hand, argued his supporters, there was no denying that Churchill's long career had equipped him with a uniquely broad grasp of military and political affairs.

Eventually on 1 September Churchill found himself back in the Cabinet and, when war was declared two days later, he found out that he was once more to be given the role of First Lord of the Admiralty. Within hours of his appointment the British liner *Athenia* was torpedoed and sunk by a German submarine in the Atlantic. It was a harbinger of what was to follow. With no significant battlefield confrontation between Germany and the Allies on the Western Front, and the enormous bombing raids feared by both sides failing to materialise, the battle for supremacy in the seas would prove central to the prosecution of the war in its opening months.

Churchill relished his new-found responsibility and threw himself into the fray with an all-consuming energy. He was full of schemes and stratagems, firing off memos that strayed well beyond his brief, and demonstrating a remarkable appetite for the smallest details. Perhaps most significantly he found himself given a much more public platform from which to exercise his singular power for oratory.

In regular Sunday evening radio broadcasts – and in the chamber of the House of Commons – he bristled with an energy and confidence that no other public figure could match. From the very first day of the war, his forthright delivery – coupled with the remarkable momentum of his return to prominence – had people talking about him as a possible prime minister in waiting. At no point was this more pronounced than on 26 September when both Chamberlain and Churchill addressed the House of Commons, with the former's funereal style utterly eclipsed by the latter's ebullience.

But, for Churchill's critics, no amount of rhetorical flair would be sufficient, on its own, to wipe the slate clean. Suspicions remained about his loyalty to the government, his predilection for 'wild schemes' and his enthusiastic interference in the fine detail of military and diplomatic affairs. The last thing that many Whitehall insiders wanted to see was his ascension to the highest office in the land – a turn of events that had seemed almost inconceivable at the beginning of the year.

Previous Page
Winston Churchill with Lord Halifax, 1938.

8 JANUARY

'I cannot feel that after all I have said,
they can be able to swallow me —
it wd [sic] have to be "horns & all".
But I can truthfully say
I do not mind.'

*Churchill in a letter to his wife Clementine, commenting
on the chances of a return to government*

14 MARCH

'I have been out of office now for
ten years, but I am more contented with
the work I have done in these last
five years … than of any other part
of my public life. I know it has gained
for me a greater measure of goodwill
from my fellow countrymen than
I have ever previously enjoyed.'

*Churchill in an address to critics in his constituency
seeking to replace him as MP*

'THE DANGER IS NOW VERY NEAR...
MILLIONS OF MEN ARE BEING
PREPARED FOR WAR. EVERYWHERE
THE FRONTIER DEFENCES ARE MANNED.
EVERYWHERE IT IS FELT THAT SOME
NEW STROKE IS IMPENDING. IF IT
SHOULD FALL, **CAN THERE BE ANY
DOUBT THAT WE SHALL BE INVOLVED?'**

Churchill in a speech in the House of Commons

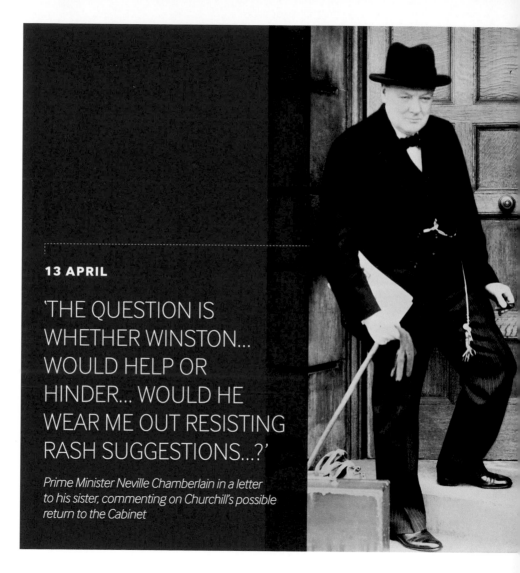

13 APRIL

'THE QUESTION IS WHETHER WINSTON... WOULD HELP OR HINDER... WOULD HE WEAR ME OUT RESISTING RASH SUGGESTIONS...?'

Prime Minister Neville Chamberlain in a letter to his sister, commenting on Churchill's possible return to the Cabinet

18 APRIL

No public man in our time has shown more foresight, and I believe that his long, lonely struggle to expose the dangers of the dictatorships will prove to be the best chapter in his crowded life.'

Churchill's long-time ally, Brendan Bracken

20 APRIL

'If the British Empire is fated to pass from life into history, we must hope it will not be by the slow processes of dispersion and decay, but in some supreme exertion for freedom, for right and for truth.'

Churchill in a speech delivered at the Canada Club

'The House, expecting, half hoping, half fearing, that it would be Winston, was amazed.'

Diary entry by Conservative MP Sir Henry Channon on the news that Chamberlain had not chosen Churchill for a new Cabinet position

Churchill on the steps of the Admiralty in Whitehall, London, in 1939.

Neville Chamberlain makes a brief speech announcing 'Peace for our Time' on his arrival at Heston Airport after his meeting with Hitler at Munich, 30 September 1938.

German troops entering the Castle District (Hradčany) in Prague, March 1939.

14 JUNE

'I FOR ONE WOULD WILLINGLY LAY DOWN MY LIFE IN COMBAT, RATHER THAN, IN FEAR OF DEFEAT, SURRENDER TO THE MENACES OF THESE MOST SINISTER MEN.'

Churchill's pre-war views on surrender – as recorded by Conservative MP Harold Nicolson

28 JUNE

'There are two supreme obligations which rest upon a British government. They are of equal importance. One is to strive to prevent a war, and the other is TO BE READY IF WAR SHOULD COME.'

Churchill in an address to the City Carlton Club

6 JULY

'Churchill is the only Englishman Hitler is afraid of... The mere fact of giving him a leading Ministerial post would convince Hitler that we really meant to stand up to him.'

A view expressed privately by Hitler's Finance Minister Count Lutz Schwerin von Krosigk, according to a Foreign Office report

8 JULY

'If Winston got into the Government, it would not be long before we were at war.'

Prime Minister Neville Chamberlain in a letter to his sister

9 JULY

'Today the *Daily Telegraph* produces a full leader... demanding the inclusion of Winston Churchill in the Government. It is quite threatening, and the PM is taken aback by it...'

Diary entry by Conservative MP Sir Henry Channon

Prime Minister Neville Chamberlain's War Cabinet. Churchill can be seen in the back row, behind the then Prime Minister.

27 JULY

'I keep thinking of Winston Churchill... full of patriotism and ideas for saving the Empire. A man who knows you must act to win. You cannot remain supine and allow yourself to be hit indefinitely. Winston must be chafing at the inaction.'

General William Edmund 'Tiny' Ironside, shortly to become the head of the British Army

2 AUGUST

'This is an odd moment for the House to declare that it will go on a two months' holiday.'

Churchill speaking against the motion that Parliament take its summer recess – just as tensions in Europe are reaching breaking point

8 AUGUST

'There is a hush over all Europe, nay, over all the world...
It is the hush of suspense, and in many lands it is the
hush of fear. Listen! No, listen carefully; I think I hear
something – yes there it was quite clear. Don't you hear
it? It is the tramp of armies crunching the gravel of the
parade-grounds, splashing through rain-soaked fields,
the tramp of two million German soldiers and more than
a million Italians – "going on manoeuvres" – yes, only
on manoeuvres! Of course it's only manoeuvres – just
like last year... Besides these German and Italian armies
may have another work of Liberation to perform. It was
only last year that they liberated Austria from the horrors
of self-government. It was only in March they freed the
Czechoslovak Republic from the misery of independent
existence... No wonder the armies are tramping on when
there is so much liberation to be done, and no wonder
there is a hush among all the neighbours of Germany
and Italy while they are wondering which one is going
to be "liberated" next.'

Churchill in a radio broadcast to the people of the USA

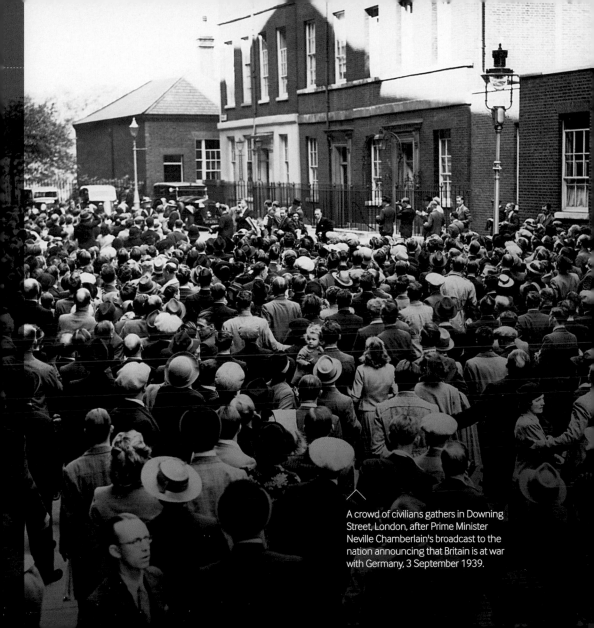

A crowd of civilians gathers in Downing Street, London, after Prime Minister Neville Chamberlain's broadcast to the nation announcing that Britain is at war with Germany, 3 September 1939.

'I THINK I SEE WINSTON EMERGING AS PM OUT OF IT BY THE END OF THE YEAR.'

Diary entry by Conservative MP Leo Amery

6 SEPTEMBER

'Today I watched Winston whispering to the PM... He is behaving well, but their deep mutual antagonism must sooner or later flare up and make co-operation impossible.'

Conservative MP Sir Henry Channon makes a diary entry on Churchill's conduct in Parliament

Prime Minister Neville Chamberlain raises his hat to the crowd as he leaves 10 Downing Street on the day that Britain declared war on Germany, 3 September 1939.

Churchill talks to Commander-in-Chief of the British Expeditionary Force, Field Marshal John Gort, at Chateau de Couroy near Avesnes, France, on 5 November 1939.

14 SEPTEMBER

'I am told that Winston is already driving the Admiralty to distraction by his interference and energy.'

Conservative MP Sir Henry Channon

24 SEPTEMBER

'During the last three weeks I have not had a minute to think of anything but my task. They are the longest three weeks I have ever lived.'

Churchill in a letter responding to a request that he write articles for a national newspaper

Royal Navy Officers watch the sinking of SS *Athenia*, 3 September 1939.

26 SEPTEMBER

'A tour-de-force, a brilliant bit of acting and exposition... he must have taken endless trouble with his speech... We must watch out.'

Diary entry by Conservative MP and Chamberlain supporter Sir Henry Channon

'The Prime Minister gets up to make his statement... One feels the confidence and spirits of the House dropping inch by inch. When he sits down there is scarcely any applause. During the whole speech Winston Churchill had sat hunched beside him... and then he gets up. He is greeted by a loud cheer from all the benches and he starts to tell us about the Naval position... THE EFFECT OF WINSTON'S SPEECH WAS INFINITELY GREATER THAN COULD BE DERIVED FROM ANY READING OF THE TEXT. HIS DELIVERY WAS REALLY AMAZING and he sounded every note from deep preoccupation to flippancy, from resolution to sheer boyishness. One could feel the spirits of the House rising with every word. It was quite obvious afterwards that the Prime Minister's inadequacy and lack of inspiration had been demonstrated even to his warmest supporters. In those twenty minutes Churchill brought himself nearer the post of Prime Minister than he has ever been before. In the Lobbies afterwards even Chamberlainites were saying, "We have now found our leader."'

Diary entry by Conservative MP Harold Nicolson

'IT WAS FOR HITLER TO SAY WHEN THE WAR WOULD BEGIN; BUT IT IS NOT FOR HIM OR FOR HIS SUCCESSORS TO SAY WHEN IT WILL END. IT BEGAN WHEN HE WANTED IT, AND IT WILL END ONLY WHEN WE ARE CONVINCED THAT HE HAS HAD ENOUGH.'

Churchill in his first wartime radio broadcast to the nation

'Heard Winston Churchill's inspiring speech... He certainly gives one confidence and will, I suspect, be Prime Minister before the war is over. Nevertheless, judging from his record of untrustworthiness and instability, he may in that case lead us into the most dangerous paths. But he is the only man in the country who commands anything like universal respect, and perhaps with age he has become less inclined to undertake rash adventures.'

Diary entry by Jock Colville, Junior Private Secretary to Prime Minister Neville Chamberlain

Survivors from the sinking
of SS *Athenia*.

2 OCTOBER

'I pray that such a catastrophe will be averted.'

Publisher Sir Ernest Benn in a letter to chancellor Sir John Simon, commenting on the idea of Churchill as prime minister

12 NOVEMBER

'The whole world is against Hitler and Hitlerism... Even in Germany itself there are millions who stand aloof from the seething mass of criminality and corruption constituted by the Nazi Party machine. Let them take courage amid perplexities and perils, for it may well be that the final extinction of a baleful domination will pave the way to a broader solidarity of all the men in all the lands than we could ever have planned if we had not marched together through the fire.'

Churchill in another of his regular radio broadcasts

13–14 NOVEMBER

'VERY BOASTFUL... OVER CONFIDENT AND INDISCREET... Winston's speech has made a very bad effect at No. 10.'

Diary entry by Jock Colville, Junior Private Secretary to Prime Minister Neville Chamberlain

19 NOVEMBER

'Tiresome letter from Winston... He ought to have enough of his own to do without butting into other people's business.'

Diary entry by Sir Alexander Cadogan, head of the Foreign Office

7 DECEMBER

'Don't irritate them dear!'

Churchill gives a sarcastic summary of the legal objections to his proposal to place mines in the Rhine

Churchill as First Lord of the Admiralty in Paris, November 1939.

16 DECEMBER

'Humanity, rather than legality,
must be our guide.'

*Churchill in a memorandum arguing that
Britain should occupy areas of neutral Norway
to prevent iron ore reaching Germany*

18 DECEMBER

'Rough and violent times lie ahead but everything that has happened since the beginning of this war should give the nation confidence that in the end the difficulties will be surmounted, the problems solved and duty done.'

Churchill in a radio broadcast announcing the sinking of the German pocket battleship Graf Spee

'I wish you could talk to us every night!'

Conservative MP Vyvyan Adams in a letter to Churchill

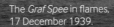

The *Graf Spee* in flames, 17 December 1939.

'THE MAN, AND THE ONLY MAN WE HAVE, FOR THIS HOUR'

After cutting a divisive and frustrated figure in Chamberlain's War Cabinet, Churchill takes over as prime minister at a time of unparalleled crisis for the nation.

'I have nothing to offer but blood, toil, tears and sweat.' So said Winston Churchill in his first speech as prime minister on 13 May 1940. He could also have added 'words', for it was in this year that his oratory seared itself into the nation's collective memory. In the coming weeks alone, he would talk of fighting on the beaches and never surrendering; he would exhort his fellow Britons to live 'their finest hour'; and he would acknowledge the debt owed by 'so many to so few'.

Perhaps his words burned so brightly because they were delivered at such a dark time in the nation's history. Churchill became prime minister on 10 May – the day that Hitler launched his lightning offensive in the Low Countries. Before the end of the month, Luxembourg, Belgium and Holland had been overrun, British troops were being evacuated from Dunkirk, France was on the verge of surrender, and the new Prime Minister was being urged by his War Cabinet to negotiate a peace.

At the start of the year, the idea that the prime minister should face such a choice was inconceivable. And that the prime minister should be Churchill would have filled Whitehall insiders with despair. 'Too belligerent', 'ineffective', 'harmful', 'useless', 'dangerous' and likely to 'bugger up the whole war'. This is how Churchill was described by politicians, civil servants and military leaders in the weeks immediately before his appointment, when his desire to take the initiative in the war brought him into conflict with his colleagues.

Towards the end of 1939, Churchill had become fixated with cutting off Germany's access to Swedish iron ore, which made its way to the country by sea via the Norwegian port of Narvik. He began by proposing that neutral Norwegian waters be mined so that ships carrying iron ore to Germany would be forced out into the open sea where they could be sunk. In making this proposal, at least, he was well within his brief as First Lord of the Admiralty. However, he went on to suggest an expedition to Narvik and an advance over land into Sweden to occupy the ore fields.

It was a proposal that served to reinforce all the prejudices that had greeted Churchill on his return to the War Cabinet. Where he saw purpose, positivity and opportunity, others saw only ambition, recklessness and risk. As discussion of his ideas dragged on into 1940, Churchill became increasingly frustrated by what he perceived to be a systemic failure of decision-making. And since he was not one to hide his feelings,

tensions in Whitehall began to run high.

Eventually, in March, the War Cabinet agreed to a limited expedition to mine Norwegian waters and occupy Narvik. But by the time the operation began in April, it was too late – German troops had themselves marched into Norway and occupied Narvik. It was a humiliating setback for the British and it put Prime Minister Neville Chamberlain's position under threat.

Events came to a head on 7 May when the House of Commons began a debate on the government's handling of the war. Shaken by what he heard, Chamberlain held private discussions over the next two days with his two potential successors: Churchill and the Foreign Minister Lord Halifax. Chamberlain's preferred candidate was Halifax but the peer was reluctant to take the job. And so it was to Churchill that the mantle fell.

The decision about whether Britain should negotiate a peace was the subject of tense discussions in the five-man War Cabinet from 26 to 28 May – just as the struggle to evacuate the British Expeditionary Force from Dunkirk was getting under way. Churchill was for fighting, but Halifax was against. What is striking about the contemporary accounts of this fraught period is just how important Churchill's words were – both in public and in private. Perhaps the most important came in an address he made to the more junior members of his government on 28 May in an attempt to out-flank Halifax. 'If this long island story of ours is to end at last,' he said, 'let it end only when each one of us lies choking in his own blood upon the ground.' They were strong, inspiring words and they had the desired effect. Britain would fight on.

The Battle of Britain raged in the skies over southern England, the threat of invasion loomed and then receded as the Royal Air Force gained the upper hand, and the Blitz began with wave after wave of German bombers subjecting Britain's cities to nightly assault. Throughout it all, Churchill acted as a rallying point for the country. His popularity with the public reached new heights, and his critics began to be won over. Not every speech went down well. Not every suspicion was lifted. Not every relationship ran smoothly. But his authority was unquestioned, and his galvanising effect acknowledged by all. Gradually, as the end of the year approached, his speeches took on a new tone. It was no longer a question of immediate survival; it was time to wage war.

Previous page
Winston Churchill at his seat in the Cabinet Room at No. 10 Downing Street, London, 1940.

10 JANUARY

'I am appalled... it is clear that the same brain who conceived the Dardanelles Campaign is responsible for this wild enterprise.'

Conservative MP Sir Henry Channon makes a diary entry about the idea of sending an expeditionary force to Sweden

15 JANUARY

'I see such immense walls of prevention, all built or building, that I wonder whether any plan will have a chance of climbing over them... One thing is absolutely certain... victory will never be found by taking the line of least resistance.'

Churchill vents his frustration in a letter to Lord Halifax

27 JANUARY

'Come then: let us to the task, to the battle, to the toil – each to our part, each to our station. Fill the armies, rule the air, pour out the munitions, strangle the U-boats, sweep the mines, plough the land, build the ships, guard the streets, succour the wounded, uplift the downcast, and honour the brave. **LET US GO FORWARD TOGETHER** in all parts of the Empire, in all parts of the Island. There is not a week, nor a day, nor an hour to lose.'

Churchill in a speech delivered in Manchester, later broadcast on the radio

'A first-rate "fighting" speech... He is indeed an orator – perhaps the only one in the country today ... Nevertheless he is a dangerous person unless kept well in control...'

Diary entry by Jock Colville, Junior Private Secretary to Prime Minister Neville Chamberlain

"LET US
GO FORWARD
TOGETHER"

37

31 JANUARY

'BARE-FACED WITH NO CAPACITY FOR THOUGHT.'

Hitler's view of Churchill according to a diary entry by Josef Goebbels, Nazi Minister for Propaganda and Public Enlightenment

2 FEBRUARY

'History is repeating itself in an astonishing way. The same string-pulling as in the last war, the same differences between statesmen and soldiers... the same tendency to start subsidiary theatres of war, and to contemplate wild projects!'

A thinly veiled reference to Churchill in a diary entry by General Sir Alan Brooke, a commander in the British Expeditionary Force

30 MARCH

'More than a million German soldiers... are drawn up ready to attack, at a few hours' notice, all along the frontiers of Luxembourg, of Belgium and of Holland. At any moment these neutral countries may be subjected to an avalanche of steel and fire; and the decision rests in the hands of a haunted, morbid being, who, to their eternal shame, the German peoples in their bewilderment have worshipped as a god.'

Churchill in a radio broadcast to the nation

Winston Churchill at
10 Downing Street for the
8am Cabinet meeting called
following the German invasion
of Holland, Belgium and
Luxembourg, 10 May 1940.

Churchill leaving 10 Downing Street, 10 May 1940.

12 APRIL

'We must get the PM to take a hand in this before Winston and Tiny [Ironside, the Chief of the Imperial General Staff] go and bugger up the whole war.'

View expressed by Sir James Grigg, Permanent Secretary at the War Office, according to a diary entry by Jock Colville

17 APRIL

'Winston has been presiding over innumerable committees, TALKING A LOT AND GETTING NOTHING DONE.'

Diary entry by Jock Colville, Chamberlain's Junior Private Secretary

25 APRIL

'He has now thrown off his mask, and is plotting against
Neville, whom up to now he has served loyally; he
wants to run the show himself: all this was inevitable,
and I am only surprised it did not come before.'

Conservative MP Sir Henry Channon confides in his diary

'The country believes that Winston is the man of
action who is winning the war and little realise how
ineffective, and indeed harmful, much of his energy
is proving itself to be...'

Diary entry by Jock Colville, Chamberlain's Junior Private Secretary

8 MAY

'I GATHER DEBATE WILL WEAKEN GOVT. BUT WHAT ARE WE TO PUT IN ITS PLACE? WINSTON USELESS...'

*Diary entry by Sir Alexander Cadogan, Chief Diplomatic
Adviser to the Foreign Secretary, following a debate in the
House of Commons about the botched Norway campaign*

9 MAY

'I thought Winston was a better choice [for PM]. Winston did not demur.'

Foreign Secretary Lord Halifax on his conversation with Chamberlain and Churchill over who should become prime minister

Churchill inspects a 'Tommy gun' while visiting coastal defence positions near Hartlepool, 31 July 1940.

10 MAY

'I AM AFRAID IT *MUST* BE WINSTON... He may, of course, be the man of drive and energy the country believes him to be... but it is a terrible risk, it involves the danger of rash and spectacular exploits, and I cannot help fearing that this country may be manoeuvred into the most dangerous position it has ever been in... EVERYBODY HERE IS IN DESPAIR AT THE PROSPECT.'

Diary entry by Jock Colville, Chamberlain's Junior Private Secretary

'The substitution of Churchill for Chamberlain is received here with absolute indifference; by the Duce with irony.'

Diary entry by Count Galeazzo Ciano, Italian Foreign Minister

'[ROOSEVELT] SUPPOSED CHURCHILL WAS THE BEST MAN THAT ENGLAND HAD, EVEN IF HE WAS DRUNK HALF OF HIS TIME.'

Diary entry by Harold Ickes, US Secretary of the Interior

Winston Churchill's Coalition Cabinet in May 1940: left to right, front row: Sir John Anderson, Winston Churchill, Clement Attlee, Anthony Eden; back row: Sir Stafford Cripps, Ernest Bevin, Lord Beaverbrook, Herbert Morrison.

13 MAY

'I HAVE NOTHING TO OFFER BUT BLOOD, TOIL, TEARS AND SWEAT...

You ask, what is our policy, I will say: It is to wage war, by sea, land and air, with all our might and with all the strength that God can give us: to wage war against a monstrous tyranny, never surpassed in the dark, lamentable catalogue of human crime. That is our policy. You ask, What is our aim? I can answer in one word: Victory — victory at all costs, victory in spite of all terror, victory, however long and hard the road may be; for without victory, there is no survival.'

Churchill in his first speech to Parliament as prime minister

19 MAY

'This is one of the most awe-striking periods in the long history of France and England... behind us – behind the armies and fleets of Britain and France – gather a group of shattered States and bludgeoned races: the Czechs, the Poles, the Norwegians, the Danes, the Dutch, the Belgians – upon all of whom the long night of barbarism will descend, unbroken even by a star of hope, unless we conquer, as conquer we must; as conquer we shall.

Today is Trinity Sunday. Centuries ago words were written to be a call and a spur to the faithful servants of Truth and Justice: "Arm yourselves, and be ye men of valour, and be in readiness for the conflict; for it is better for us to perish in battle than to look upon the outrage of our nation and our altar. As the Will of God is in Heaven, even so let it be."'

Churchill in his first radio broadcast as prime minister

'I thought things must be hopeless when Mr Churchill started quoting Scripture.'

Mrs White, cook to Violet Bonham Carter, a noted liberal and friend of Churchill – as recorded in a diary entry by Bonham Carter

'Whatever Winston's shortcomings, he seems to be the man for the occasion. His spirit is indomitable and even if France and England should be lost, I feel he would carry on the crusade himself with a band of privateers. Perhaps my judgements of him have been harsh, but the situation was very different a few weeks ago.'

Diary entry by Jock Colville, now appointed Private Secretary to Churchill and clearly warming to his new master

Winston Churchill half length portrait.

27 MAY

'We had a long and rather confused discussion about... general policy in the event of things going really badly in France. I thought Winston talked the most frightful rot... It does drive one to despair when he works himself up into a passion of emotion when he ought to make his brain think and reason.'

Lord Halifax confides in his diary following a fraught meeting of the War Cabinet to discuss whether Britain should fight on or not in the event of the fall of France

28 MAY

'If this long island story of ours is to end at last, let it end only when each one of us lies choking in his own blood upon the ground.'

Churchill to his ministers seeking support for his policy of fighting on, as recorded in a diary entry by Hugh Dalton, Labour MP and Minister of Economic Warfare

'HE IS QUITE MAGNIFICENT. THE MAN, AND THE ONLY MAN WE HAVE, FOR THIS HOUR.'

A further diary entry by Dalton

31 MAY

'The King... has had to remind Winston that he is only PM in England and not in France as well!'

Diary entry by Labour MP Hugh Dalton on Churchill's desire to influence events on the continent

4 JUNE

'Even though large tracts of Europe and many old and famous States have fallen or may fall into the grip of the Gestapo and all the odious apparatus of Nazi rule, we shall not flag or fail. We shall go on to the end, we shall fight in France, we shall fight on the seas and the oceans, we shall fight with growing confidence and growing strength in the air, **WE SHALL DEFEND OUR ISLAND, WHATEVER THE COST MAY BE, WE SHALL FIGHT ON THE BEACHES, WE SHALL FIGHT ON THE LANDING GROUNDS, WE SHALL FIGHT IN THE FIELDS AND IN THE STREETS, WE SHALL FIGHT IN THE HILLS; WE SHALL NEVER SURRENDER...'**

Churchill in a speech to the House of Commons on the day that the operation to evacuate troops from Dunkirk came to an end

'He was eloquent, and oratorical, and used MAGNIFICENT ENGLISH; SEVERAL LABOUR MEMBERS CRIED.'

Diary entry by Conservative MP Sir Henry Channon

'A grand speech... evidently designed... to pull ostrich heads out of the sand both here and in the USA.'

Diary entry by Labour MP Hugh Dalton

'Worth 1,000 gns [sic] ... THE SPEECH OF 1,000 YEARS.'

Labour MP Colonel Josiah Wedgwood in a letter to Churchill

'I do not feel the burden weigh too heavily, but I cannot say that I have enjoyed being PM vy [sic] much so far.'

Churchill in a letter to former Prime Minister Stanley Baldwin

16 JUNE

'It is put to me that Winston is surrounded by stimulants – his "Brains Trust"... What he really needs, some think, are sedatives. He is always getting new ideas... and taking sudden decisions of great importance. Most of these are probably very good, but the Chiefs of Staff live in a constant state of terror of what he may do, or decide, without consulting them.'

Diary entry by Labour MP and government minister Hugh Dalton

British troops line up on the beach at Dunkirk to await evacuation, May 1940.

'What General Weygand called the Battle of France is over. I expect that the Battle of Britain is about to begin. UPON THIS BATTLE DEPENDS THE SURVIVAL OF CHRISTIAN CIVILISATION. Upon it depends our own British life, and the long continuity of our institutions and our Empire. The whole fury and might of the enemy must very soon be turned on us. Hitler knows that he will have to break us in this island or lose the war. If we can stand up to him, all Europe may be free and the life of the world may move forward into broad, sunlit uplands. But if we fail, then the whole world, including the United States, including all that we have known and cared for, will sink into the abyss of a new Dark Age made more sinister, and perhaps more protracted, by the lights of perverted science. LET US THEREFORE BRACE OURSELVES TO OUR DUTIES, AND SO BEAR OURSELVES THAT, IF THE BRITISH EMPIRE AND ITS COMMONWEALTH LAST FOR A THOUSAND YEARS, MEN WILL STILL SAY, "**THIS WAS THEIR FINEST HOUR.**"'

Churchill in a speech to the House of Commons, later delivered again over the radio

'I wasn't very impressed, but I suppose that the nation will be.'

Diary entry by Conservative MP Sir Henry Channon

'How I wish Winston would not talk on the wireless unless he is feeling in good form. He hates the microphone... Now, as delivered in the House of Commons, that speech was magnificent, especially the concluding sentences. But it sounded ghastly on the wireless. All the great vigour he put into it seemed to evaporate.'

Conservative MP Harold Nicolson in a letter to his wife

20 JUNE

'His command of English is magnificent; but strangely enough, although he makes me laugh, he leaves me unmoved. There is always the quite inescapable suspicion that he loves war, war which broke Neville Chamberlain's better heart.'

Diary entry by Conservative MP Sir Henry Channon

22 JUNE

'Everyone all over the place and WSC endorses any wild idea.'

Diary entry by Sir Alexander Cadogan, Chief Diplomatic Adviser to the Foreign Secretary

Supermarine Spitfire Mark IAs of No 610 Squadron, Royal Air Force, based at Biggin Hill, Kent, July 1940.

'My Darling, I hope you will forgive me if I tell you something that I feel you ought to know.

One of the men in your entourage (a devoted friend) has been to me & told me that there is a danger of your being generally disliked by your colleagues & subordinates because of your rough sarcastic & overbearing manner – It seems your Private Secretaries have agreed to behave like schoolboys & "take what's coming to them" & then escape out of your presence shrugging their shoulders – Higher up, if an idea is suggested (say at a conference) you are supposed to be so contemptuous that presently no ideas, good or bad, will be forthcoming. I was astonished & upset because in all these years I have been accustomed to all those who have worked with & under you, loving you – I said this & I was told "No doubt it's the strain" –

My Darling Winston – I must confess that I have noticed a deterioration in your manner; & you are not so kind as you used to be.

It is for you to give the Orders & if they are bungled – except for the King and the Archbishop of Canterbury & the Speaker you can sack anyone & everyone – Therefore with this terrific power you must combine urbanity, kindness and if possible Olympic calm… I cannot bear that those who serve the Country & yourself should not love you as well as admire and respect you –

Besides you won't get the best results by irascibility & rudeness. They will breed either dislike or a slave mentality – (Rebellion in War time [*sic*] being out of the question!)

Please forgive your loving devoted
& watchful Clemmie

(I wrote this at Chequers last Sunday,
tore it up, but here it is now.)'

A letter from Clementine to Churchill

Winston and Clementine on
the Thames, viewing bomb
damage to the docks on
25 September 1940.

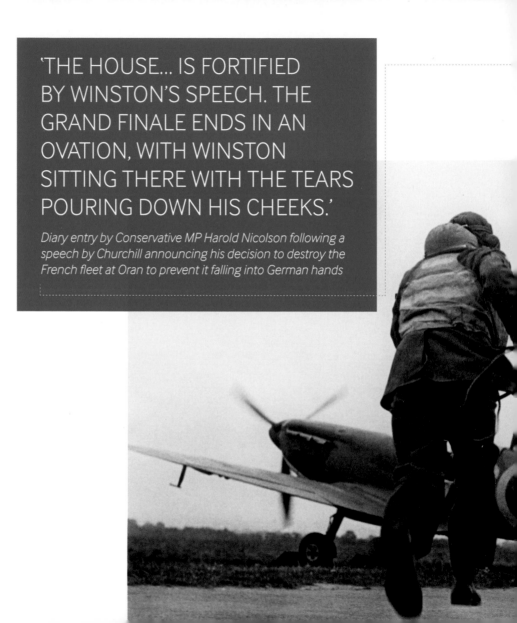

'THE HOUSE... IS FORTIFIED BY WINSTON'S SPEECH. THE GRAND FINALE ENDS IN AN OVATION, WITH WINSTON SITTING THERE WITH THE TEARS POURING DOWN HIS CHEEKS.'

Diary entry by Conservative MP Harold Nicolson following a speech by Churchill announcing his decision to destroy the French fleet at Oran to prevent it falling into German hands

12 JULY

'[Winston] emphasised that the great invasion scare... is serving a most useful purpose: it is well on the way to providing us with the finest offensive army we have ever possessed and it is keeping every man and woman tuned to a high pitch of readiness. He does not wish the scare to abate therefore, and although personally he doubts whether invasion is a serious menace he intends to give that impression, and to talk about long and dangerous vigils, etc., when he broadcasts on Sunday.'

Diary entry by Churchill's Private Secretary Jock Colville

Pilot of No. 64 Squadron RAF running towards his Supermarine Spitfire Mark 1A as the Squadron is scrambled at Kenley, 10.45am, 15 August 1940.

'And now it has come to us to stand alone in the breach, and face the worst that the tyrant's might and enmity can do... We await undismayed the impending assault. Perhaps it will come to-night. Perhaps it will come next week. Perhaps it will never come. We must show ourselves equally capable of meeting a sudden violent shock, or what is perhaps a harder test, a prolonged vigil. But be the ordeal sharp or long, or both, we shall seek no terms, we shall tolerate no parley; we may show mercy — we shall ask for none...'

Churchill in a radio address to the nation

'I clapped when it was over. But really he has got guts, that man. Imagine the effect of his speech in the Empire and the USA... What a speech!'

Conservative MP Harold Nicolson in a letter to his wife

22 JULY

'AND NOW, GO AND SET EUROPE ABLAZE.'

Churchill's instruction to minister Hugh Dalton after giving him responsibility for the new Special Operations Executive – as recorded in Dalton's diary

'He is most interesting to listen to and full of the most marvellous courage, considering the burden he is bearing. He is full of offensive thoughts for the future, but I think he fully realises the difficulties he is up against.'

Diary entry by General Sir Alan Brooke, newly appointed Commander-in-Chief of Britain's Home Forces, after dining with Churchill at Downing Street

Churchill meets infantrymen manning a coast defence position near Hartlepool on 31 July 1940.

24 JULY

'I do not propose to say anything in reply to Herr Hitler's speech, not being on speaking terms with him.'

A note handwritten by Churchill in the margin of one of his papers

30 JULY

'HE NOW LEADS THE WHOLE HOUSE, UNQUESTIONED AND ASCENDANT.'

Diary entry by Labour MP and government minister Hugh Dalton

10 AUGUST

'[Winston] could not quite see why he appeared to be so popular. After all since he came into power, everything had gone wrong and he had nothing but disasters to announce.'

Diary entry by Churchill's Private Secretary Jock Colville

Poster issued in honour of RAF's Fighter Command after its victory in the Battle of Britain. It features Churchill's famous tribute to 'The Few', 20 August 1940.

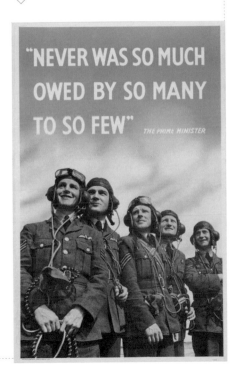

20 AUGUST

'The gratitude of every home in our Island, in our Empire, and indeed throughout the whole world, except in the abodes of the guilty, goes out to the British airmen who, undaunted by odds, unwearied in their constant challenge and mortal danger, are turning the tide of the world war by their prowess and by their devotion. **NEVER IN THE FIELD OF HUMAN CONFLICT WAS SO MUCH OWED BY SO MANY TO SO FEW.'**

Churchill in a speech to the House of Commons, as the Battle of Britain continues to rage

20 AUGUST

'For the first time in a year I read an English speech which is definite and forward-looking... Behind the façade of beautiful words and strong affirmations there is a will and a faith.'

Diary entry by Count Galeazzo Ciano, Italian Foreign Minister

'Nothing so simple, so majestic and so true has been said in so great a moment of human history. You have beaten your old enemies "the Classics" into a cocked hat!'

Violet Bonham Carter in a letter to Churchill

27 AUGUST

'Every night... I try myself by court martial to see if I have done anything effective during the day. I don't mean just pawing the ground; anyone can go through the motions; but something really effective.'

A remark by Churchill to his Private Secretary Jock Colville, as recorded in Colville's diary

29 AUGUST

'I am honoured to sit at the same table with a man who so closely resembles Jesus Christ, but I want to win the war.'

Churchill's response when Frank Pick, the Director-General of the Ministry of Information, expressed his determination to deal only in the truth

Churchill studies reports of the action that day with Vice Admiral Sir Bertram Ramsay, Flag Officer Commanding Dover, on 28 August 1940.

Winston Churchill viewing activity in the Channel from an observation post at Dover Castle during his tour of defences, 28 August 1940.

Churchill sings with a group of Australian troops at Tidworth, Hampshire, during his visit to the camp on 4 September 1940.

11 SEPTEMBER

'IF THIS INVASION IS GOING TO BE TRIED AT ALL, IT DOES NOT SEEM THAT IT CAN BE LONG DELAYED... EVERY MAN AND WOMAN WILL THEREFORE PREPARE HIMSELF TO DO HIS DUTY, WHATEVER IT MAY BE, WITH SPECIAL PRIDE AND CARE....'

Churchill in a radio broadcast to the nation

'Today my wife heard the inspiring address of Mr Churchill. He is a truly wonderful leader and you are fortunate to have such a man at the head of government. More power to him.'

American Richard E Taylor in a letter to a British friend

'Brilliant, inspiring but just a tiddly bit frightening.'

Maria Blewitt, a member of the Women's Auxiliary Air Force, in a letter home

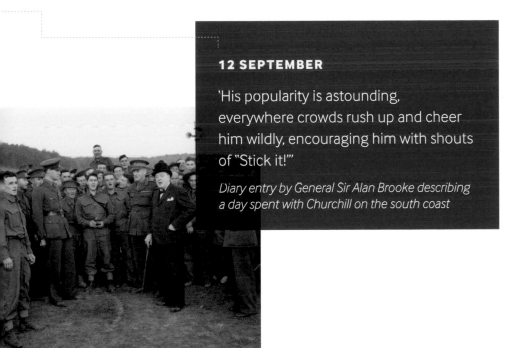

12 SEPTEMBER

'His popularity is astounding, everywhere crowds rush up and cheer him wildly, encouraging him with shouts of "Stick it!"'

Diary entry by General Sir Alan Brooke describing a day spent with Churchill on the south coast

'ON EVERY SIDE, THERE IS THE CRY, "WE CAN TAKE IT," BUT WITH IT, THERE IS ALSO THE CRY, "GIVE IT 'EM BACK."'

Churchill in a speech to Parliament

'Somewhat subdued ... he seems to be having a devil of a bad time.'

Diary entry by Josef Goebbels, Nazi Minister for Propaganda and Public Enlightenment

11 OCTOBER

'[The PM] has a wonderful vitality and bears his heavy burden remarkably well. It would be impossible to find a man to fill his place at present.'

Diary entry by General Sir Alan Brooke, Commander-in-Chief of Britain's Home Forces

23 OCTOBER

'Remember, it isn't only the good boys who help to win wars; it is the sneaks and the stinkers as well.'

Churchill remarking on the desirability of employing General Percy Hobart, who was unpopular with his military superiors

27 OCTOBER

'Young Winston, Randolph's son, ... is absurdly like his grandfather; but, as one of the daughters said, "so are all babies".'

John Martin, Churchill's Private Secretary, in a letter to his mother

Churchill awaits a train as he continues his tour of coastal defences, 23 October 1940.

3 NOVEMBER

'To watch [Churchill] compose some telegram or minute for dictation is to make one feel that one is present at the birth of a child, so tense is his expression, so restless his turnings from side to side, so curious the noises he emits under his breath. Then comes out some masterly sentence and finally with a "Gimme" he takes the sheet of typewritten paper and initials it or alters it with his fountain pen, which he holds most awkwardly halfway up the holder.'

Diary entry by Churchill's Private Secretary Jock Colville

Visiting bombed out buildings in the East End of London on 8 September 1940.

5 NOVEMBER

'By putting the grim side foremost he impresses us with his ability to face the worst. He rubs the palms of his hands with five fingers extended up and down the front of his coat, searching for the right phrase, indicating cautious selection, conveying almost medicinal poise. If Chamberlain had spoken glum words such as these the impression would have been one of despair and lack of confidence. Churchill can say them and we all feel, "Thank God that we have a man like that!" I have never admired him more.'

Conservative MP Harold Nicolson in his diary

9 NOVEMBER

'BETWEEN IMMEDIATE SURVIVAL AND LASTING VICTORY THERE IS A LONG ROAD TO TREAD.'

Churchill in a speech delivered at the annual Lord Mayor's Luncheon in London

14 NOVEMBER

'ALWAYS STAND UP TO HIM. HE HATES DOORMATS. IF YOU BEGIN TO GIVE WAY HE WILL SIMPLY WIPE HIS FEET UPON YOU.'

*Advice from Lord Halifax on how to handle Churchill,
as recorded in a diary entry by Labour MP Hugh Dalton*

21 NOVEMBER

'Up to the present this war has been waged between a fully-armed Germany and a quarter- or half-armed British Empire. We have not done so badly. I look forward with confidence and hope to the time when we ourselves shall be as well armed as our antagonists...'

Churchill in a speech to the House of Commons

25 NOVEMBER

'WINSTON TURNED UP IN A GREY ROMPER
SUIT. IT WAS ALL I COULD DO TO KEEP MY FACE
STRAIGHT... He talked from 9.30 to 12, round
and round and across. It is quite shattering to
me the love to talk some people have.'

*Lord Halifax makes an entry in his diary about
a meeting with Churchill*

26 DECEMBER

'The Prime Minister has made a great point of working as usual over the holiday and yesterday morning was like almost any other here, with the usual letters and telephone calls... From lunchtime on less work was done... It was the same after dinner. For once the shorthand-writer was dismissed and we had a sort of sing-song until after midnight. The PM sang lustily, if not always in tune, and... danced a remarkably frisky measure of his own in the middle of the room. He then sat up and talked till 2am; but I still found him as brisk as ever this morning.'

John Martin, Churchill's Private Secretary, in a letter to his mother

Standing out of the flames and
smoke of surrounding blazing
buildings, St Paul's Cathedral during
the great fire raid in London,
24 December 1940.

'A FEW SCRATCHES ARE STARTING TO SHOW'

As the first year of Churchill's premiership draws to a close and the second begins, he has little success with which to bolster confidence in his government.

At the beginning of 1941, Britain was a country under siege. For over three months, its cities and ports had been pulverised by enemy bombs, while at sea its supply lines were being slowly severed by the ruthless efficiency of Germany's submarines. Yet, in comparison to the imminent threat of invasion in the summer of 1940, these months represented a period of invaluable breathing space. Work continued apace to strengthen the country's defences and to rebuild its fighting force, but there was chance too to consider questions of wider strategy.

After the tumult and chaos of his first few months in office, Churchill had settled on what was, to him at least, a more agreeable way to run the war. Now, every decision was made with his direct involvement, either in his capacity as prime minister or in the job he had created for himself as minister for defence. In his public and private utterances, and in remarks made about him by colleagues, he cuts a confident figure, energised by the responsibilities he had assumed.

The key challenge that he set himself was to wage a prolonged and careful campaign to court US support. It was a campaign in which his rhetorical skills mattered. He aimed speech after speech at American ears: some delivered directly in the presence of US officials in the UK; others over the airwaves to President Roosevelt, who was known to be listening in the White House. He played on themes of shared values and history, and probed for ways to make it easier for Roosevelt to join the war.

These subtle and eloquent overtures were made against a backdrop of deepening gloom. In February, the progress that British troops had made against Italian forces in North Africa was halted by the arrival of German reinforcements. In April and May, German forces conquered Yugoslavia, Greece and Crete, in the latter two cases occasioning a humiliating withdrawal of British troops. And all the while, the Blitz continued to wreak havoc at home.

Partly for the benefit of the watching Americans, but also to rally the beleaguered public, Churchill embarked on a series of journeys around the country. Visiting cities such as Liverpool, Bristol, Manchester, Cardiff and Swansea, he demonstrated a keen sense of how he had come to embody Britain's spirit of defiance. He made frequent public appearances on foot and in slow car rides, making impromptu speeches and waving his signature hat and cigar. Everywhere he went he appears to have been greeted with genuine warmth,

affection and respect.

Nonetheless, Churchill was not immune to the deluge of bad news that flooded in from every front. Not quite a year into office, he was forced to defend his government against a vote of confidence tabled in the House of Commons, and rumblings of unrest continued into the summer months.

Lurking beneath some of this discontent it is possible to detect growing friction between the Prime Minister and his Chiefs of Staff – the professional heads of the Army, Navy and Air Force. He appears to have been frustrated by their caution, and they by his impatience.

Two developments seem to have arrested this slump in Churchill's popularity. The first was Hitler's decision to launch an invasion of the Soviet Union on 22 June, which meant that Britain no longer stood alone in the war against Germany, and seemed less likely to suffer an invasion of its own. The second was the meeting that Churchill managed to engineer between himself and President Roosevelt off the shores of Newfoundland in August. It brought no immediate practical benefit, but it allowed Churchill to speak with more confidence in public about the prospect of US support.

Privately, however, Churchill, knew better than anyone that his words would not be sufficient to bring America into the war. For that, something else would have to happen – something momentous.

He did not have to wait long. On 7 December Japan launched a surprise attack on the US fleet at Pearl Harbor and, to Churchill's barely concealed delight, Germany followed by making its own declaration of war, so drawing the US into the European conflict.

However, as Churchill journeyed across the Atlantic once more to meet his new and much longed-for ally, he left behind a scene of discontent at home. Britain may have found an ally but she had also gained a powerful and frighteningly effective enemy in Japan. Confidence in Churchill's government remained fragile and it was soon going to get worse. Much worse.

Previous page
Franklin D Roosevelt and Winston Churchill on board HMS *Prince of Wales* in the North Atlantic during the Atlantic Conference, 10 August 1941.

Left
Churchill speaking to merchant ships' crews and dockers in Liverpool, thanking them for their part in fighting the Battle of the Atlantic, c.25 April 1941.

9 JANUARY

'I... hail it as a most fortunate occurrence that at this awe-striking climax in world affairs there should stand at the head of the American Republic a famous statesman, long versed and experienced in the work of government and administration, in whose heart there burns the fire of resistance to aggression and oppression, and whose sympathies and nature make him the sincere and undoubted champion of justice and of freedom, and of the victims of wrong-doing wherever they may dwell.'

Churchill comments on the re-election of President Roosevelt

11 JANUARY

'Mr Hopkins paid a graceful tribute to the PM's speeches which had, he said, produced the most stirring and revolutionary effect on all classes and districts in America. At an American Cabinet meeting the President had had a wireless set brought in so that all might listen to the Prime Minister. The PM was touched and gratified. He said that he hardly knew what he said in his speeches last summer; he had just been imbued with the feeling that "it would be better for us to be destroyed than to see the triumph of such an imposter".'

Churchill's Private Secretary Jock Colville makes a diary entry describing a meeting between Churchill and US envoy Harry Hopkins

24 JANUARY

'The PM said... he now woke up in the mornings, as he nearly always had, feeling as if he had a bottle of champagne inside him and glad that another day had come. In May and June, however, he had been sorry when the nights were over and he had often thought about death.'

Diary entry by Churchill's Private Secretary Jock Colville

Churchill raises his hat in salute during an inspection of the 1st American Squadron of the Home Guard at Horse Guards Parade, London, 9 January 1941.

'THE HOUR HAS COME; KILL THE HUN.'

Churchill on how he would end his speech if ever he had to announce a German invasion, as recorded in Jock Colville's diary

FEBRUARY

'[Churchill is] the directing force behind the strategy and conduct of the war in all its essentials. HE HAS AN AMAZING HOLD ON THE BRITISH PEOPLE OF ALL CLASSES AND GROUPS.'

Assessment of Churchill by Harry Hopkins, adviser to President Roosevelt

9 FEBRUARY

'Here is the answer which I will give to President Roosevelt: Put your confidence in us. Give us your faith and your blessing, and, under providence, all will be well. We shall not fail or falter; we shall not weaken or tire. Neither the sudden shock of battle, nor the long-drawn trials of vigilance and exertion will wear us down. Give us the tools, and we will finish the job.'

Churchill in a radio address to Britain and the Empire.

'First-rate... triumphant and yet not over-optimistic, addressed very largely to American ears.'

Churchill's Private Secretary Jock Colville reacts to the speech in his diary

'Insolent and certain of victory. At the height of his illusory triumph.'

Diary entry by Josef Goebbels, Nazi Minister for Propaganda and Public Enlightenment

Churchill, Clementine and Harry Hopkins are welcomed by dockyard workers on board the battleship HMS *Queen Elizabeth*.

THE PRIME MINISTER

"In the next few months we shall have a gap to fill. It is particularly necessary that all munition workers, all those who are engaged in war industries, should make a further effort proportionate to the magnitude of the perils and the magnitude of our cause. Particularly does this apply to TANKS and

ABOVE ALL TO AIRCRAFT

Aircraft will be more than ever necessary now that the war has spread over so many wide spaces of the earth."

AVENGE OUR BATTLESHIPS

MINISTRY OF AIRCRAFT PRODUCTION.

Propaganda poster using Churchill's powerful oratory, published 1941.

26 FEBRUARY

'It is terrifying. If it goes on it will be the end of us.'

Churchill's private reaction to the news that more Allied ships had been sunk in the Atlantic

2 MARCH

'I have an uneasy feeling that when things get very bad there may be a movement in this country to attribute the whole disaster to "the war-mongers" and to replace Churchill by... some appeaser.'

Diary entry by Conservative MP Harold Nicolson

5 MARCH

'The poor Chiefs of the Staff will get very much out of breath in their desire to run away.'

Churchill privately bemoaning military advice to withdraw Allied troops from Greece

12 APRIL

'There had been a bad raid during the night and many of the ruins were still smoking. The people looked bewildered but... were thrilled by the sight of Winston who drove about sitting on the hood of an open car and waving his hat.'

Churchill's Private Secretary Jock Colville makes a diary entry about a visit by the Prime Minister to Bristol

23 APRIL

'Now Churchill is even being attacked in the London press. A few scratches are starting to show... After all Mr Churchill's loud trumpetings, there is silence.'

Diary entry by Josef Goebbels, Nazi Minister for Propaganda and Public Enlightenment

27 APRIL

'**To leave the offices in Whitehall with their ceaseless hum of activity and stress, and to go out to the front, by which I mean the streets and wharves of London or Liverpool, Manchester, Cardiff, Swansea or Bristol, is like going out of a hothouse on to the bridge of a fighting ship. It is a tonic... What a triumph the life of these battered cities is, over the worst that fire and bomb can do... All are proud to be under the fire of the enemy... This is indeed the grand heroic period of our history, and THE LIGHT OF GLORY SHINES ON ALL.**'

Churchill in a broadcast address to the nation

'IT MAY HAVE GONE DOWN VERY WELL WITH THE 99 PER CENT WHO KNOW NOTHING, BUT THE 1 PER CENT OF US WHO DO KNOW, FEEL RATHER DIFFERENTLY.'

Remark made by Conservative MP Oliver Stanley, as recorded in a diary entry by Labour MP Hugh Dalton

Churchill is cheered by workers during a visit to bomb-damaged Plymouth on 2 May 1941.

3 MAY

'A book on Churchill reports that he drinks too much and wears pink silk underwear. He dictates messages in the bath or in his underpants; a startling image which the Führer finds hugely amusing.'

Diary entry by Josef Goebbels, Nazi Minister for Propaganda and Public Enlightenment

Churchill signs the visitors' book in Birkenhead, Merseyside, April 1941.

7 MAY

'My right honourable Friend [Mr Lloyd George] spoke of the great importance of my being surrounded by people who would stand up to me and say "No, No, No." Why, good gracious, has he no idea how strong the negative principle is in the constitution and working of the British war-making machine? The difficulty is not, I assure him, to have more brakes put on the wheels; the difficulty is to get more impetus and speed behind it.'

Churchill answering criticism of his government ahead of a vote of confidence

'Pungent, amusing, cruel, hard-hitting... he tore his opponents to shreds... but in reality the Government has been shaken and... Winston [knows] it.'

Conservative MP Sir Henry Channon in his diary

27 MAY

'He is quite the most wonderful man I have ever met, and is a source of never ending interest studying and getting to realize that occasionally such human beings make their appearance on this earth. Human beings who stand out head and shoulders above all others.'

Diary entry by General Sir Alan Brooke, then Commander-in-Chief of the Home Forces

Churchill speaks during a tank demonstration in Luton, 23 May 1941.

6 JUNE

'On all sides one hears increasing criticism of Churchill. He is undergoing a noticeable slump in popularity and many of his enemies, long silenced by his personal popularity, are once more vocal.'

Diary entry by Conservative MP Sir Henry Channon

10 JUNE

'If the Government has always to be looking over its shoulder to see whether it is going to be stabbed in the back or not, it cannot possibly keep its eye on the enemy.'

Churchill addressing growing unrest in the House of Commons

16 JUNE

**'United we stand.
Divided we fall.
Divided, the dark age returns.
United, we can save and guide the world.'**

Churchill in a radio speech to America

18 JUNE

'The man has something... But for him, the war would have been over long ago.'

Diary entry by Josef Goebbels, Nazi Minister for Propaganda and Public Enlightenment

'If Hitler invaded Hell [I] would at least make a favourable reference to the Devil.'

Churchill, an arch anti-Communist, on supporting Russia in the event of a German invasion, as recorded in the diary of his Private Secretary, Jock Colville

Taking aim with a Sten gun during a visit to the Royal Artillery experimental station at Shoeburyness in Essex, 13 June 1941.

Waffen- SS motorcyclists lead a column of German troops during the advance into the Soviet Union, 1941.

23 JUNE

'MAKE HELL WHILE THE SUN SHINES.'

Churchill privately toying with the idea of an attack on the French coast now that Germany was busy fighting in Russia

25 JUNE

'Do not let anyone suppose that inside this
enormous Government we are a mutual
admiration society. I do not think, and my
colleagues will bear me witness, any expression
of scorn or severity which I have heard used
by our critics, has come anywhere near the
language I have been myself accustomed to
use, not only orally, but in a continued stream
of written minutes. In fact, I WONDER THAT
A GREAT MANY OF MY COLLEAGUES ARE ON
SPEAKING TERMS WITH ME... If we win, nobody
will care. If we lose, there will be nobody to care.'

Churchill in a secret session of the House of Commons

14 JULY

'YOU DO YOUR WORST — AND WE WILL DO OUR BEST.'

Churchill, in an address to a lunch organised by the London County Council, voicing the response that Londoners would like to give to Hitler

Churchill walks past a four-engined Boeing Fortress Mark I at a Bomber Command Station, 6 June 1941.

22 JULY

'Interminable speeches by PM... NO DECISIONS ARE TAKEN NOR PROPER PLANS THOUGHT OUT.'

Foreign Secretary Anthony Eden commenting privately on the functioning of the War Cabinet and Defence Committee

25 JULY

'He drove in my car between troops lining both sides of the road. All of them cheering him as he went and shouting "Good Old Winnie". HIS POPULARITY IS QUITE ASTONISHING.'

General Sir Alan Brooke, Commander-in-Chief of the Home Forces

29 JULY

'Few of his usual oratorical tricks. Someone has told him that we are weary of his eloquence.'

Conservative MP Sir Henry Channon makes a diary entry responding to a speech by Churchill on war production

3 AUGUST

'HE MAY HAVE TO GO IF WE ARE TO WIN THE WAR.'

Diary entry by Foreign Office official Oliver Harvey

Roosevelt and Churchill on board USS *Augusta*, 9 August 1941.

24 AUGUST

'That is the message of the Atlantic meeting... Help is coming; mighty forces are arming in your behalf. Have faith. Have hope. Deliverance is sure.'

Churchill in a broadcast following his meeting with President Roosevelt in Newfoundland

9 SEPTEMBER

'This is no time for boasts or glowing prophecies but there is this – a year ago our position looked forlorn and well nigh desperate to all eyes but our own. Today we may say aloud before an awe-struck world, "We are still masters of our fate. We still are captains of our souls."'

Churchill ends a speech in Parliament on the war situation with a quote from the poem 'Invictus' by William Ernest Henley

'His speech has a good effect, and the slight anti-Churchill tide which had begun to be noticeable was checked.'

Conservative MP Harold Nicolson reacts to Churchill's speech in his diary

26 SEPTEMBER

'The PM *will* give the V sign with two fingers in spite of the representations repeatedly made to him that this gesture has quite another significance... The drive back to the station was a triumphant procession. The crowds stood on the pavements, as thick as for the opening of Parliament in London, for miles and miles along the route. They waved, they cheered, they shouted: every face seemed happy and excited. I have seen the PM have many enthusiastic receptions but never one equal to this. It is clear that his name and fame are as great today as they have ever been. He was deeply moved.'

Churchill's private secretary Jock Colville describes a visit to Coventry in his diary

30 SEPTEMBER

'Nothing is more dangerous in wartime than to live in the temperamental atmosphere of a Gallup Poll, always feeling one's pulse and taking one's temperature... If today I am very kindly treated by the mass of the people of this country, it is certainly not because I have followed public opinion in recent years. There is only one duty, only one safe course, and that is to try to be right and not to fear to do or say what you believe to be right. That is the only way to deserve and to win the confidence of our great people in these days of trouble.'

Churchill on the relationship between his popularity and his policies, in a speech to the House of Commons

26 OCTOBER

'He had the gramophone turned on and in his many coloured dressing gown, with a sandwich in one hand and water cress in the other, he trotted round and round the hall giving occasional little skips... On each lap near the fireplace he stopped to release some priceless quotation or thought.'

General Sir Alan Brooke, Commander-in-Chief of the Home Forces, makes a diary entry describing a late-night encounter with Churchill at Chequers

Churchill gives his famous 'V for Victory' sign while addressing crowds from the balcony of City Hall in Sheffield, during a tour of the Midlands and North of England, 6–8 November 1941.

Churchill during a tour of the dock area of Liverpool in late September 1941.

29 OCTOBER

'NEVER GIVE IN, NEVER GIVE IN, NEVER, NEVER, NEVER, NEVER — IN NOTHING, GREAT OR SMALL, LARGE OR PETTY — NEVER GIVE IN EXCEPT TO CONVICTIONS OF HONOUR AND GOOD SENSE...'

Churchill in a speech to the boys of Harrow School

12 NOVEMBER

'It is a month ago that I remarked upon the long silence of Herr Hitler, a remark which apparently provoked him to make a speech in which he told the German people that Moscow would fall in a few days. That shows, as everyone, I am sure will agree, how much wiser he would have been to go on keeping his mouth shut...'

Comments made by Churchill in a speech to mark the opening of a new session of Parliament.

16 NOVEMBER

'I have the greatest respect... and real affection for him, so that I hope I may be able to stand the storms of abuse which I may well have to bear frequently.'

Diary entry by General Sir Alan Brooke reacting to his promotion to Chief of the Imperial General Staff (the professional head of the British Army) – and his likely relationship with Churchill

4 DECEMBER

'We were told that we did nothing but obstruct his intentions, we had no ideas of our own, and whenever he produced ideas we produced nothing but objections... GOD KNOWS WHERE WE WOULD BE WITHOUT HIM, BUT GOD KNOWS WHERE WE SHALL GO WITH HIM!'

General Sir Alan Brooke makes an entry in his diary describing a fractious meeting between Churchill and the Chiefs of Staff

Churchill addresses a joint session of the US Congress on 26 December 1941 in Washington DC.

US President Franklin D Roosevelt signs the declaration of war against Japan following the aerial bombardment of Pearl Harbor, December 1941.

8 DECEMBER

'When we look around us over the sombre panorama of the world, we have no reason to doubt the justice of our cause or that our strength and will-power will be sufficient to sustain it... In the past we have had a light which flickered, in the present we have a light which flames, and in the future there will be a light which shines over all the land and sea.'

Churchill in a speech to the House of Commons following the Japanese attack on the US fleet at Pearl Harbor

11 DECEMBER

'Victory is traditionally elusive. Accidents happen. Mistakes are made. Sometimes right things turn out wrong, and quite often wrong things turn out right. War is very difficult...'

Churchill in a speech to Parliament

18 DECEMBER

'The Government... is doomed: I give it a few months. No Government could survive such unpopularity for long.'

Diary entry by Conservative MP Sir Henry Channon

26 DECEMBER

'I cannot help reflecting that if my father had been an American and my mother British, instead of the other way round, I might have got here on my own.'

Churchill on being invited to give a speech in the United States Senate Chamber in Washington

Churchill addresses the Canadian
Parliament in Ottawa, December 1941.

'ONE NIGHT I SHALL NOT RETURN'

Disaster follows disaster in the early months of 1942, putting Churchill's own position at risk. Both he and Britain will need success before the year is out.

If 1940 was about Britain's fight for survival and 1941 about its need for allies, then 1942 could be said to be about Churchill's survival as prime minister and his desperate need for any kind of military success. Although Japanese aggression had brought the US into the war, it had also resulted in a series of damaging defeats in British territories in the Far East. When Churchill returned to Britain from Washington in January 1942, he was met with serious discontent. Over two years into the war and continental Europe was overrun by Germany, the British Army had enjoyed no lasting success anywhere on the globe, and, as Churchill himself would later put it, every ocean bar the Atlantic was in enemy hands.

This time criticism of the government was not limited to the House of Commons, where once again Churchill was forced to dig into his rhetorical armoury to fend off another vote of confidence. In February he was attacked for the first time in the national press, which had been stung by the surrender of Singapore – one of the jewels in Britain's imperial crown – and outraged by the fact that two German warships had managed to steam untouched along the English Channel in an escape run back to Germany. This was a humiliation too far and provoked such a storm of protest that Churchill was forced to make changes to his War Cabinet.

Churchill was aware too that his own position was in jeopardy and that his personal popularity would only carry him so far. 'I am like a bomber pilot,' he said in private in April, 'I go out night after night, and I know that one night I shall not return.' It was a striking analogy – all the more so given that the RAF had that same month launched its systematic, concentrated, and controversial, 'area bombing' of German cities.

In June came the bad news that the North African town of Tobruk had fallen to the Germans – news made all the more humiliating by being delivered to Churchill while he was in a meeting with President Roosevelt at the White House. 'Now for England,' the Prime Minister said as he departed Washington, 'home, and a beautiful row.'

There followed another debate in the House of Commons criticising the 'central direction of the war' and once again Churchill managed to get through it, but unless things changed, it appeared that he was living on borrowed time. What he needed was a victory and he decided to take a more direct role in securing it, flying out to Cairo, Moscow and Tehran to bring his personal influence to bear on the course of events.

Churchill had long been dissatisfied by the way that the war was being fought in the Middle East and he was determined not only to shake up the command of the Army in North Africa but also to speak directly to the soldiers themselves. By the time he returned to Britain in September, he had appointed a new Commander-in-Chief, General Harold Alexander, and a new Commander of the Eighth Army, General Bernard Montgomery. He had also talked extensively with them about a new offensive against the Afrika Korps troops commanded by the 'Desert Fox' General Erwin Rommel, and the subsequent British-American landings planned in North Africa that November known as Operation 'Torch'.

Then the talking was over, and there followed the part that Churchill always seemed to find the hardest: waiting. The Prime Minister seems to have kept a deliberately low profile through the remainder of September and October, conscious that this could well constitute his final roll of the dice. 'If Torch fails, then I'm done for,' he confided in a colleague.

It did not fail. In fact the landings

were made almost unopposed. More gratifyingly still, they were preceded by a decisive victory for Montgomery's Eighth Army in a fierce battle near the town of El Alamein. This was the victory that Churchill had been craving – the victory that Britain so desperately needed. It was also the cue for a return to rhetorical form: 'Now this is not the end,' he said in a speech delivered at the Lord Mayor's Luncheon in London. 'It is not even the beginning of the end. But it is, perhaps, the end of the beginning.'

It was a well measured phrase, and it captured a new note of confidence for the future. Churchill had survived a year of personal struggle, but 1943 would bring difficulties of a new kind.

Previous page
Churchill at the controls of a Boeing 314 flying boat, January 1942.

1 JANUARY

'Here's to 1942, here's to a year of toil — a year of struggle and peril, and a long step forward towards victory. May we all come through safe and with honour.'

New Year toast by Churchill to his staff and newspaper correspondents while travelling by train from Ottawa to Washington

9 JANUARY

'Every MP present [said] that the Government was doomed. It was no use, they said, the PM coming back and making one of his magical speeches... This time... the Government must be reformed.'

Diary entry by Conservative MP Sir Henry Channon describing the mood of fellow MPs

Churchill pictured in the White House gardens, 3 January 1942.

27 JANUARY

'When I was called upon to be Prime Minister, now nearly two years ago, there were not many applicants for the job. Since then, perhaps, the market has improved…

I stand by my original programme, blood, toil, tears and sweat, which is all I have ever offered, to which I added, five months later, "many shortcomings, mistakes and disappointments". But it is because I see the light gleaming behind the clouds and broadening on our path, that I make so bold now as to demand a declaration of confidence of the House of Commons…'

Churchill taking on his critics in Parliament

'One can actually feel the wind of opposition dropping sentence by sentence, and by the time he finishes it is clear that there is really no opposition at all – only a certain uneasiness.'

Diary entry by Conservative MP Harold Nicolson

29 JANUARY

'When at last the figures [for the vote of confidence] are announced – 464 to 1 – there [is] a faint cheer. The victory is a triumph for Churchill, though there was no alternative and he knows it. Nevertheless HE IS THE MOST INSPIRING LEADER WE HAVE, AND THE MASSES AND THE AMERICANS BOTH ADORE HIM.'

Conservative MP Sir Henry Channon makes an entry in his diary describing the atmosphere in the House of Commons after the vote of confidence

9 FEBRUARY

'Our army is the mockery of the world. Then about 130,000 tons of shipping sunk in a week! Poor Winston v. desperate.'

Diary entry by Sir Alexander Cadogan, Chief Diplomatic Adviser to the Foreign Secretary

11 FEBRUARY

'Singapore must certainly fall very soon if it has not already done so. Churchill's star seems to be on the wane.'

Diary entry by Liverpool local government official W A Rodgers

Churchill inspects a guard of honour at Greenwich Naval College, 1942.

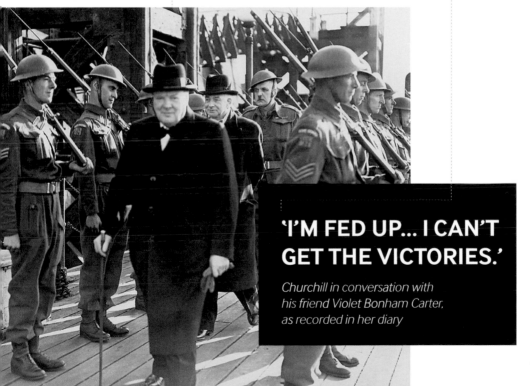

'I'M FED UP... I CAN'T GET THE VICTORIES.'

Churchill in conversation with his friend Violet Bonham Carter, as recorded in her diary

13 FEBRUARY

'A violently anti-Churchill, anti-Government leader in the *Daily Mail*. It is the first that has ever appeared. EVERYONE IS IN A RAGE AGAINST THE PRIME MINISTER... Rage; frustration. This is not the post-Dunkirk feeling, but ANGER.'

Diary entry by Conservative MP Sir Henry Channon on the reaction to a series of defeats and setbacks in every theatre of the war

14/15 FEBRUARY

'Nothing less than the departure of Winston... will now avail. Poor Winston... after all that he has done for the country.'

Diary entry by Foreign Office official Oliver Harvey

Churchill at an inspection of 9th Armoured Division near Newmarket, Suffolk, 16 May 1942.

15 FEBRUARY

'Many misfortunes, severe torturing losses, remorseless and gnawing anxieties lie before us... This, therefore, is one of those moments when the British race and nation can show their quality and their genius... We must remember that we are no longer alone. We are in the midst of a great company. Three quarters of the human race are now moving with us... So far we have not failed. We shall not fail now. Let us move forward steadfastly together into the storm and through the storm.'

Churchill in his first broadcast address for nearly six months

'His broadcast... was not liked. The country is too nervous and irritable to be fobbed off with fine phrases. Yet what else could he have said?'

Conservative MP Harold Nicolson reacts to the broadcast in his diary

17 FEBRUARY

'Never have I known the House growl at a Prime Minister... He was obviously disgruntled and shaken... I felt sorry for him.'

Diary entry by Conservative MP Sir Henry Channon

24 FEBRUARY

'While... I take constitutional responsibility for everything that is done or not done, and am quite ready to take the blame when things go wrong [...] I do not think there has ever been a system in which the professional heads of the Fighting Services have had a freer hand or a greater or more direct influence, or have received more constant and harmonious support from the Prime Minister and the Cabinet under which they serve.'

Churchill in a speech to the House of Commons explaining changes to his Cabinet and answering criticisms about how he conducts the war

27 FEBRUARY

'The new Cabinet stocks are going up and those
of the PM going down, and... before long the
younger men... will take over. PM does seem
to be losing both grip and ground; he is quite
exhausted by his superhuman efforts.'

Diary entry by Foreign Office official Oliver Harvey

'I CANNOT BEAR THE THOUGHT
THAT THIS HEROIC FIGURE
SHOULD NOW BE SNIPED
AT BY TINY LITTLE MEN.'

Diary entry by Conservative MP Harold Nicolson

26 MARCH

'When we look back over the sombre year that has passed, and forward to the many trials that lie before us, no one can doubt for a moment the improvement in our war position. A year ago we were alone: now three of the greatest nations in the world are sworn to us in close alliance... it now seems very likely that we and our allies... cannot lose this war.'

Churchill tries to stem growing doubts about Britain's prospects in a speech to the Conservative Party

'AN ORATOR OF SINGULAR POWER, CAPABLE OF MOVING PEOPLE DEEPLY.'

Diary entry by Count Galeazzo Ciano, Italian Foreign Minister

22 APRIL

'I am like a bomber pilot... I go out night after night, and I know that one night I shall not return.'

Churchill remarking on the decline in his popularity, as recorded in the diary of Conservative MP Harold Nicolson

Churchill inspecting the Parliamentary Home Guard, London, 13 May 1942.

23 APRIL

'For nearly two hours the PM spoke with almost no interruption; it was a tour de force [...] We left the Chamber confident that the War would, after all, be won...'

Diary entry by Conservative MP Sir Henry Channon

11 MAY

'I was on watch last night for Churchill's speech but he gives me the pip anyway so I didn't miss much. I don't need him to give me moral support and if a vote was cast in the services for him he would not be there anyway, the Navy has a special dislike of him as we do all his dirty work for him.'

Able Seaman Christopher Gould in a letter home from the Far East

16 MAY

'Here in the 33rd month of the War none of us is weary of the struggle. None of us is calling for any favours from the enemy. If he plays rough we can play rough too. Whatever we have got to take we will take, and we will give it back in even greater measure.'

Churchill in a speech to the public in Leeds

1 JULY

'That this House, while paying tribute to the heroism and endurance of the Armed Forces of the crown in circumstances of exceptional difficulty, has no confidence in the central direction of the war.'

A motion moved for debate in the House of Commons

Churchill makes a radio
address from his desk
at 10 Downing Street,
June 1942.

2 JULY

'Everything that could be thought-of or raked-up has
been used to weaken confidence in the Government, has
been used to prove that Ministers are incompetent and to
weaken their confidence in themselves, to make the Army
distrust the backing it is getting from the civil power, to
make the workmen lose confidence in the weapons they are
striving so hard to make, to represent the Government as
a set of nonentities over whom the Prime Minister towers,
and then to undermine him in his own heart and, if possible,
before the eyes of the nation... Do not, I beg you, let the
House underrate the gravity of what has been done...'

Churchill mounts his defence in Parliament

3 JULY

'PM made, as usual, a great speech yesterday and on the whole seems to have won the sympathy of the House. All were rather overawed by the issues being fought out in Africa and slightly ashamed of themselves.'

Diary entry by Foreign Office official Oliver Harvey

8 JULY

'We'd better put an advertisement in the papers, asking for ideas.'

Churchill expressing frustration at what he perceived as the inaction of his Chiefs of Staff, as recorded in a diary entry by Sir Alexander Cadogan, Chief Diplomatic Adviser to the Foreign Secretary

31 JULY

'Why does Churchill never seem to say or do anything nowadays? What is he waiting for?'

British housewife Elizabeth Belsey in a letter to her serviceman husband

Churchill at Alamein, 7 August 1942.

30 JULY

'[The PM] is to start tomorrow for Egypt ... But what energy and gallantry of the old gentleman, setting off at 65 across Africa in the heat of mid-summer!'

Diary entry by Foreign Office official Oliver Harvey

'When things are going well, [Winston] is good; when things are going badly, he is superb; but when things are going half-well, he is "hell on earth".'

General Hastings Ismay, Churchill's Chief of Staff, as recorded in a diary entry by Conservative MP Harold Nicolson

9 AUGUST

'I intend to see every important unit in this army, both back and front and make them feel the vast consequences that depend on them and the superb honour which may be theirs.'

Churchill writes to his wife from the British Embassy in Cairo, explaining one of the key aims of his journey to North Africa

Churchill wearing his world famous siren suit, pictured with the son of the British Ambassador in the gardens of the British Embassy, Cairo, Egypt on 8 August 1942.

Churchill during his second visit to the Western Desert, 23 August 1942.

8 SEPTEMBER

**'We are sea animals, and the United States are to a large extent ocean animals.
The Russians are land animals.
Happily, we are all three air animals...'**

Churchill speaking in the House of Commons

29 SEPTEMBER

'WE SHALL LOSE THE WAR IF CHURCHILL STAYS.'

A remark by Labour MP Aneurin Bevan, as recorded in the diary of Conservative MP Harold Nicolson

A rare colour photograph records Churchill's visit to the Home Fleet on 11 October 1942. To his left is Admiral Sir John Tovey, Commander-in-Chief Home Fleet; to the right is the Lord Privy Seal Sir Stafford Cripps.

2 OCTOBER

'IF TORCH FAILS, THEN I'M DONE FOR.'

Churchill on the forthcoming operation to land Allied troops in North Africa, as recorded in the diary of Foreign Office official Oliver Harvey

12 OCTOBER

'Our enemies have been more talkative lately... There is one note which rings through all these speeches; it can be clearly heard above their customary boastings and threats — the dull, low, whining note of fear... [Hitler] sees with chagrin and amazement that our defeats are but stepping-stones to victory, and that his victories are only the stepping-stones to ruin.'

Churchill speaking in Edinburgh

10 NOVEMBER

'Now... we have a new experience. We have victory —
a remarkable and definite victory. The bright gleam
has caught the helmets of our soldiers, and warmed
and cheered all our hearts... NOW THIS IS NOT THE
END. IT IS NOT EVEN THE BEGINNING OF THE END.
BUT IT IS, PERHAPS, THE END OF THE BEGINNING.'

Churchill speaking after the Battle of El Alamein

American troops exit their landing craft on the beach near Oran, Algeria, as part of Operation 'Torch', November 1942.

Churchill, cigar in mouth, gives his famous 'V' for victory sign during a visit to Bradford, 4 December 1942.

11 NOVEMBER

'For 76 minutes we had a dramatic treat as [Winston] described the African landings, the victory in Egypt etc... It was a creditable, indeed amazing, performance, for an overworked man of 68... The announcement that the Church bells are to be rung on Sunday in celebration of the Egyptian victory, was enthusiastically received.'

Diary entry by Conservative MP Sir Henry Channon paying tribute to Churchill's return to oratorical form

29 NOVEMBER

'The ceaseless flow of good news from every theatre of war, which has filled the whole month of November, confronts the British people with a new test. They have proved that they can stand defeat; they have proved that they can bear with fortitude and confidence long periods of unsatisfactory and unexplained inaction. I see no reason why we should not show ourselves equally resolute, and active in the face of victory...'

Churchill in a radio address to the world

30 NOVEMBER

'A hard taskmaster, and the most difficult man to serve that I have ever met, but IT IS WORTH ALL THESE DIFFICULTIES TO HAVE THE PRIVILEGE TO WORK WITH SUCH A MAN.'

Diary entry about Churchill by General Sir Alan Brooke, Chief of the Imperial General Staff

10 DECEMBER

'In war it is not always possible to have everything go exactly as one likes. In working with allies it sometimes happens that they develop opinions of their own.'

Remark made by Churchill during a secret session of the House of Commons

14 DECEMBER

'IT WAS GRAND TO HEAR HIS VOICE AND FEEL THAT YOU WERE ALL PROBABLY LISTENING TOO.'

Servicewoman Francie Brown reacts to one of Churchill's broadcasts in a letter home from overseas

A poster designed for the War Office by Frank Newbould in 1942 to present an idealised version of a Britain worth fighting for.

'THE STRAIN OF PROTRACTED WAR'

A year of travelling, conferences, planning and decision-making exacts a physical toll on Churchill, and brings him into private conflict with his closest colleagues.

The long-awaited military success achieved at the end of 1942 brought a new challenge for Churchill. In directing the course of the war, it was no longer a question of arresting the enemy's momentum, but of taking the fight forwards. It was a task that required Churchill to look beyond the requirements of the here and now, and to plan instead for the longer term. And that in turn meant daring to look at the possible post-war world, factoring in political as well as military considerations, and – perhaps most complicatedly of all – finding a way to exert meaningful influence on his Allies.

And so it was that 1943 began with a conference in Casablanca, attended primarily by the British and Americans, but with French leaders also involved. The timing was significant. The British and Americans were buoyed by the success of Operation 'Torch', while the watching Soviets were on the verge of forcing a German surrender at Stalingrad. High on the agenda was the question of when the western Allies would launch an invasion of northern France, which the Soviets hoped would draw German strength away from the East. The Soviets naturally wanted this 'Second Front' to be opened up as quickly as possible, and the Americans were inclined to agree, but Churchill had other ideas. He and his advisers believed that it would be better to press home the advantage established in North Africa so that the Allies could strike into mainland Europe through

Sicily and Italy. An invasion of northern France could then be launched sometime in 1944.

The Casablanca Conference gave Churchill a grand stage on which to perform and he appears to have revelled in the role. Backed up by a large and well prepared entourage, he succeeded in carrying the day on the question of the Second Front, and boarded the plane back to London in high spirits. Days after his return, however, he was laid low by a severe bout of pneumonia – perhaps brought on by the discomfort of flying at altitude. He was, after all, a 68-year-old man, with a penchant for the finer things in life. He had also, it seems, caught the travel bug. On recovering from his pneumonia, he went on to make two more trips across the Atlantic to hold talks with Roosevelt – journeying to Washington in May and Quebec in August.

It was during this period, after a few months of relative calm, that cracks began to appear once more in the relationship between Churchill and those around him. Churchill himself, though ebullient as ever in public, was feeling the strain of this new phase of the war in which crucial questions of strategy had to be decided. 'To have the initiative is an immense advantage,' he said, 'at the same time, it is a heavy and exacting responsibility.' It appears to have brought him into increasingly regular conflict behind the scenes with his military and political colleagues, most notably General Sir Alan Brooke, the professional head of the British Army.

Brooke had enjoyed a close relationship with the Prime Minister in his previous role as Commander-in-Chief of Britain's Home Forces, responsible for the defence of the country against a possible German invasion. He had a great deal of admiration for Churchill's abilities, but in 1943 he became increasingly frustrated with the Prime Minister's quixotic interference in matters of military planning and strategy. A similar story emerges from officials at the Foreign Office, charged with formulating and executing the concurrent diplomatic strategy. And it does not seem coincidental that from this period onwards we begin to see mutterings about post-war

come the private criticisms, and it is hard not to see a link between Churchill's evident distemper during this period, the stresses of his position, and the fact that he ended the year with another serious bout of illness.

In all he spent 31 days of 1943 confined to his sickbed with doctors sometimes fearing for his life. As the war entered what could be a decisive year, people began to wonder whether the Prime Minister would last the course.

elections – and Churchill's suitability for peacetime leadership.

On Churchill's return from Quebec in September, matters appear to have worsened. The bi-lateral discussions ended with agreement that the invasion of north-west France should be attempted in May 1944, and plans were made to hold the first ever 'Big Three' conference in Tehran in November. It was in preparation for this conference that the strain really began to tell. 'A very old man with outdated ideas', 'as jealous as a ballerina', 'less and less well balanced'

Previous page
Churchill sits in the sunshine in Marrakesh, Morocco, in December 1943 during a period of convalescence after falling ill with pneumonia.

Above
Churchill returns from his trip to Canada and the US, September 1943.

26 JANUARY

'I have never seen him in better form. He ate and drank enormously all the time, settled huge problems, played bagatelle and bezique by the hour, and generally enjoyed himself... [He] handled the situation with consummate skill.'

Harold Macmillan, newly appointed British Minister Resident in North Africa, makes a diary entry describing Churchill at the Allied Conference at Casablanca

Churchill and Roosevelt during a press conference at Villa Dar es Saada, Casablanca, 24 January 1943.

8 FEBRUARY

'PM in very belligerent mood, as usual on the return from these trips… His encounters with Roosevelt always have a bad effect. He dominates the President and at the same time envies him for being untrammelled by a Cabinet.'

Diary entry by Foreign Office official Oliver Harvey

11 FEBRUARY

'The Casablanca Conference was… unparalleled… We now have a complete plan of action… and although there will surely be disappointments and failures – many disappointments and serious failures and frustrations – there is no question of drifting or indecision, or being unable to form a scheme or waiting for something to turn up. For good or for ill, we know exactly what it is we wish to do.'

Churchill in an address to Parliament on his return from North Africa

11 MARCH

'[Roosevelt] loves Winston as a man
for the war, but is horrified at his
reactionary attitude for after the war.'

Foreign Office official Oliver Harvey in his diary

21 MARCH

'I believe myself to be what is called a good European...
We must try... to make the Council of Europe, or
whatever it may be called, into a really effective
League, with... a High Court to adjust disputes, and
with forces, armed forces, national or international
or both, held ready to impose those decisions and
prevent further aggression and the preparation
of future wars... It is my earnest hope... that we
shall achieve the largest common measure of the
integrated life of Europe that is possible without
destroying the individual characteristics and
traditions of its many ancient and historic races.'

Churchill outlines his vision for post-war Europe in a radio broadcast

'Quite an inspiring speech and will do much for morale. There was little fault even a Socialist could find with it.'

Diary entry by British signalman E A Pye

23 MARCH

'Friction is healthy, and is widely and almost universally dispersed.'

Churchill answering a question in Parliament about rumours of unrest in the government

Churchill photographed in Turkey, c.22 April 1943.

26 MARCH

'[THE PM] RECEIVED ME... LOOKING LIKE A ROMAN
CENTURION WITH NOTHING ON EXCEPT A LARGE BATH
TOWEL DRAPED AROUND HIM! He shook me warmly by
the hand in this get up and told me to sit down while he
dressed. A most interesting procedure, first he stepped
into a white silk vest, then white silk drawers, and walked
up and down the room in this kit, LOOKING RATHER
LIKE "HUMPTY DUMPTY", WITH A LARGE BODY AND
SMALL THIN LEGS! Then a white shirt which refused
to join comfortably round the neck and so was left
open with a bow tie to keep it together. Then the hair
(what there is of it!) took much attention, a handkerchief
was sprayed with scent and then rubbed over his head.
The few hairs were then brushed, and finally sprayed
direct! Finally trousers, waistcoat and coat,
and meanwhile he rippled on the whole time about
Monty's battle and our proposed visit to North Africa.'

General Sir Alan Brooke, Chief of the Imperial General Staff, in his diary

17 APRIL

'What are the elements of greatness in C's makings.
I think they are: indomitable courage, a great
memory, capacity for hard work and complete
command of the English language.'

*Diary entry by Lieutenant General Sir Charles Gairdner, Chief of Staff
to the Commander-in-Chief of Britain's forces in the Middle East*

During a visit to the
African Front, May 1943.

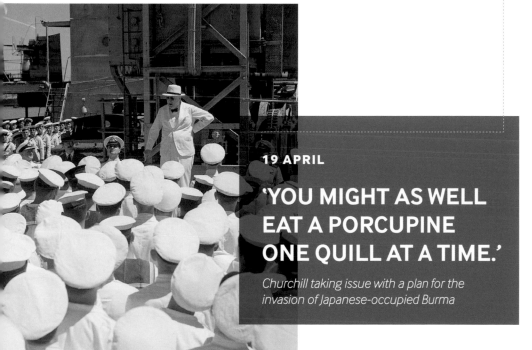

19 APRIL

'YOU MIGHT AS WELL EAT A PORCUPINE ONE QUILL AT A TIME.'

*Churchill taking issue with a plan for the
invasion of Japanese-occupied Burma*

'LOTS OF PEOPLE CAN MAKE GOOD PLANS FOR WINNING THE WAR IF THEY HAVE NOT GOT TO CARRY THEM OUT.'

Churchill in a speech to the US Congress

The Prime Minister gives the V sign on the steps of the British Embassy in Washington, May 1943.

Arriving at the House of Representatives in Washington, May 1943.

24 MAY

'And Winston??? Thinks one thing at one moment and another at another moment. At times the war may be won by bombing and all must be sacrificed to it. At others it becomes essential for us to bleed ourselves dry on the Continent because Russia is doing the same. At others our main effort must be in the Mediterranean, directed against Italy or Balkans alternatively, with sporadic desires to invade Norway and "roll up the map in the opposite direction to Hitler"! But more often than all he wants to carry out ALL operations simultaneously... !'

Diary entry by General Sir Alan Brooke, Chief of the Imperial General Staff

'IT IS HIGH TIME THE OLD MAN CAME HOME. THE AMERICAN ATMOSPHERE, THE DICTATORIAL POWERS OF THE PRESIDENT AND THE ADULATION WHICH SURROUNDS HIM THERE, HAVE GONE TO HIS HEAD.'

Diary entry by Foreign Office official Oliver Harvey

25 MAY

'We shall continue to operate on the Italian donkey at both ends, with a carrot and with a stick.'

Churchill in a press conference at the White House

8 JUNE

'TO HAVE THE INITIATIVE IS AN IMMENSE ADVANTAGE; AT THE SAME TIME, IT IS A HEAVY AND EXACTING RESPONSIBILITY.'

Churchill in a speech in the House of Commons

14 JULY

'I'm beginning to know the form now. Frightful rows, nervous exhaustion on both sides, then next day a rather contrite PM seeking to make up, like a schoolboy who knows he's been naughty, rather shamefaced, needing much face-saving. Rather winning.'

Diary entry by Foreign Office official Oliver Harvey identifying a pattern in Churchill's relationship with Foreign Secretary Anthony Eden

The Sicily landings, July 1943.

Churchill at a luncheon party given by Admiral Sir Andrew Cunningham, Commander-in-Chief to the Mediterranean Fleet, Algiers, June 1943.

16 JULY

'The time has come for you to decide whether Italians shall die for Mussolini and Hitler – or live for Italy and for civilisation.'

Extract from a joint message to the Italian people from Churchill and President Roosevelt

21 JULY

'Pure patriotic joy that my country should have found such a leader. The furnace of the war has smelted out all base metals from him.'

Former prime minister Stanley Baldwin after a visit to see his old nemesis Churchill, as recorded in the diary of Conservative MP Harold Nicolson

27 JULY

'The guilt and folly of Mussolini have cost the Italian people dear. It looked so safe and easy in May 1940 to stab falling France in the back… It looked so safe and easy to fall upon the much smaller State of Greece… Events have taken a different course…

The overthrow and casting-down in shame and ruin of the first of the dictators and aggressor war lords strikes a knell of impending doom in the ears of those that remain.'

Churchill on the fall of Mussolini in a speech to Parliament

Churchill addresses British troops in the old Roman amphitheatre at Carthage, Tunisia, on 1 June 1943.

'The most statesmanlike of his utterances… he avoided cheap jibes or wit at the expense of the fallen Duce.'

Diary entry by Conservative MP Sir Henry Channon, reacting to Churchill's speech about 'Il Duce', Mussolini

10 AUGUST

'CROWDS COLLECT WHEREVER WE STOP AND WAVE AND CHEER THE PM AND RETURN HIS V SIGN. RATHER LUDICROUS TO SEE A PRIEST GIVE THE SIGN…'

John Martin, Churchill's Private Secretary, in a letter home during a trip to Canada

23 AUGUST

'THIS AFTERNOON PM HAD SOME ICED WATER. HE TOOK A SIP AND SAID "THIS WATER TASTES VERY FUNNY." "OF COURSE IT DOES" SAID [LORD HALIFAX] "IT'S GOT NO WHISKY IN IT!"'

Diary entry by Sir Alexander Cadogan on an exchange between Churchill and Lord Halifax

23 AUGUST

'Winston made matters almost impossible, temperamental like a film star, and peevish like a spoilt child...

I wonder whether any historian of the future will ever be able to paint Winston in his true colours. It is a wonderful character – the most marvellous qualities and superhuman genius mixed with an astonishing lack of vision at times, and an impetuosity which if not guided must inevitably bring him into trouble again and again... HE IS QUITE THE MOST DIFFICULT MAN TO WORK WITH THAT I HAVE EVER STRUCK, BUT I SHOULD NOT HAVE MISSED THE CHANCE OF WORKING WITH HIM FOR ANYTHING ON EARTH!'

Diary entry by General Sir Alan Brooke, Chief of the Imperial General Staff

Churchill salutes Allied troops in the amphitheatre at Carthage, during a visit to troops near Tunis, June 1943.

'THE PRICE OF GREATNESS IS RESPONSIBILITY.'

Churchill in a speech at Harvard University

Churchill returns from Canada with Clementine, September 1943.

16 SEPTEMBER

'I said that... if we plunged back to a party fight, there was no doubt that the PM and the Tories would sweep the board. I did not think, however, that this would be good for the country.'

Labour MP and member of the coalition government Hugh Dalton in his diary

21 SEPTEMBER

'This class of criticism which I read in the newspapers when I arrived on Sunday morning reminds me of the simple tale... about the sailor who jumped into a dock... to rescue a small boy from drowning. About a week later this sailor was accosted by a woman, who asked "Are you the man who picked my son out of the dock the other night?" The sailor replied modestly, "That is true, Ma'am." "Ah," said the woman, "you are the man I am looking for. Where is his cap?"'

Churchill in a speech to the House of Commons

22 SEPTEMBER

'I was not there at the time. Perhaps it was lucky for him.'

Churchill responding to a question in the House of Commons about how the captive Mussolini was able to escape his guards

'Except for you and me, this is the worst Government England ever had!'

Churchill in conversation with Foreign Secretary Anthony Eden, as recorded in the diary of Sir Alexander Cadogan, head of the Foreign Office

29 SEPTEMBER

'WAR IS THE TEACHER, A HARD, STERN, EFFICIENT TEACHER. WAR HAS TAUGHT US TO MAKE THESE VAST STRIDES FORWARD TOWARDS A FAR MORE COMPLETE EQUALISATION OF THE PARTS TO BE PLAYED BY MEN AND WOMEN IN SOCIETY.'

Churchill in a speech to six thousand women at the Royal Albert Hall

Winston Churchill addresses American Naval and Army Cadets at Harvard University in Cambridge, Massachusetts, on 6 September 1943, on the same day as he was presented with an honorary degree by the university.

Churchill pictured in Iran on his 69th birthday, November 1943.

5 OCTOBER

'I never witnessed such deplorable proceedings. PM can be a very good leader in war time. But he *can* be the worst chairman of a Cabinet imaginable.'

Diary entry by Sir Alexander Cadogan, head of the Foreign Office

6 OCTOBER

'I'm afraid this is the usual picture before a conference. The PM has no understanding of the peace issues, and is A VERY OLD MAN WITH OUTDATED IDEAS.'

Foreign Office official Oliver Harvey confides in his diary

8 OCTOBER

'I AM SLOWLY BECOMING CONVINCED THAT IN HIS OLD AGE WINSTON IS BECOMING LESS AND LESS WELL BALANCED. I CAN CONTROL HIM NO MORE.'

Diary entry by General Sir Alan Brooke,
Chief of the Imperial General Staff

13 OCTOBER

'As soon as the war is ended, the soldiers will leave off fighting and the politicians will begin.'

Churchill in a speech to the House of Commons

Churchill en route to the Allied Conference in Cairo, November 1943.

1 NOVEMBER

'My God! The PM will lose us the war yet. His passionate and unscrupulous obstinacy is terrible and he is as jealous as a ballerina.'

Foreign Office official Oliver Harvey on Churchill's refusal to allow the Russians to participate in his next meeting with Roosevelt

9 NOVEMBER

'A great many people speak as if the end of the war in Europe were near... I am myself proceeding on the assumption that the campaign of 1944 in Europe will be the most severe, and to the Western allies, the most costly in life of any we have yet fought...'

Churchill in a speech at the Mansion House, London

153

16 NOVEMBER

'Why, you may take the most gallant sailor, the most intrepid airman, or the most audacious soldier, put them at a table together — what do you get? *The sum total of their fears!*'

Churchill privately criticises the Chiefs of Staff system

23 NOVEMBER

'NEVER FORGET THAT WHEN HISTORY LOOKS BACK YOUR VISION & YOUR PIERCING ENERGY COUPLED WITH YOUR PATIENCE & MAGNANIMITY WILL ALL BE PART OF YOUR GREATNESS. SO DON'T ALLOW YOURSELF TO BE MADE ANGRY...'

Clementine Churchill writes to her husband following a disagreement with US General Dwight D Eisenhower

9 DECEMBER

'[Stalin] has a good sense of humour, and is very adept at pulling Winston's leg. He can get a rise out of Winston... and enjoys it.'

Diary entry by Sir Alexander Cadogan,
head of the Foreign Office

Churchill with Roosevelt and Stalin at a dinner party in Tehran, held on the occasion of Churchill's 69th birthday, 30 November 1943.

15 DECEMBER

'LORD MORAN... THOUGHT THE PM WAS GOING TO DIE LAST NIGHT.'

Diary entry by Harold Macmillan, British Minister
Resident in North Africa, recording the view
of Churchill's physician the morning after the
Prime Minister apparently suffered a heart attack

16 DECEMBER

'Even at worst... he has pulled us out of the shadow and victory is certain in the not too distant future.'

Lieutenant General Sir Charles Gairdner, Chief of Staff to General Sir Harold Alexander, Commander-in-Chief Middle East, reacts to the news of Churchill's illness

25 DECEMBER

'The PM is remarkably well... The doctors are quite unable to control him and cigars etc. have now returned. I was amazed to find him dictating their bulletin. As [his personal physician] said, they have the benefit of an excellent consultant – the PM himself.'

John Martin, Churchill's Private Secretary in a letter to his mother

'He really is a remarkable man. Although he can be so tiresome and pig-headed, THERE IS NO ONE LIKE HIM. His devotion to work and duty is quite extraordinary.'

Diary entry by Harold Macmillan, British Minister Resident in North Africa

'AFTER A WEEK'S FEVER THE INTRUDERS WERE REPULSED. I HOPE ALL OUR BATTLES WILL BE EQUALLY WELL CONDUCTED.'

Churchill reports on his convalescence following his second serious bout of illness in a year.

Churchill with General Dwight D Eisenhower at his headquarters in Tunis, Tunisia, on Christmas Day 1943.

'CHAINED TO THE CHARIOT OF A LUNATIC'

Worn down by illness and less able to influence the course of an accelerating Allied war machine, Churchill struggles to conduct the everyday business of government.

On his return to Britain in mid-January, Churchill faced a period of gnawing anxiety as preparations began in earnest for the Normandy landings. It was made all the worse for a man of his restless temperament by the lack of any distractions. The time for talking had passed. There were no conferences to prepare for, no journeys to make. The plans had been set, the wheels were in motion and there was little for the Prime Minister to do but wait.

It seems too that he had yet to recover fully from his bout of illness. He made regular complaints in private about feelings of exhaustion, and this in turn seems to have exacerbated his tendency at meetings to indulge in lengthy rambling speeches rather than stick to the agenda.

For the people around him, themselves struggling under the burden of their responsibilities, his behaviour began to prove intolerable. In April the veteran head of the Foreign Office, Sir Alexander Cadogan, feared that Churchill was breaking down and in May the Prime Minister himself admitted that he would be quite happy to spend the whole day in bed.

Since the beginning of 1943, when the tide of the war had begun to turn in the Allies' favour, the thoughts of politicians, press and public alike had turned to the prospect of the post-war world. Throughout the whole of 1943, Churchill had made only one broadcast speech, in which he had outlined his vision for post-war Europe. Otherwise,

he had spent much of the year away from Britain and questions of domestic policy. He did not return to the airwaves until March 1944 – a gap of almost twelve months – and some of his physical infirmity seems to have come across in his speech, which did not come close to the rhetorical heights of four years earlier.

In the House of Commons too, cracks were beginning to appear in his coalition government, with its constituent parties jostling for position ahead of the General Election that would inevitably follow the end of the war. In April, Churchill suffered the indignity of seeing an Education Bill voted down in Parliament – the first time that his government had lost such a vote. He mounted a spirited response, but it was a battle which he would have preferred not to have had to fight.

When D-Day came on 6 June, it initially seemed to give Churchill a lift, not only because it was executed with such success, but also because it allowed him to feel closer to the action. He couldn't wait to get to the front himself and he was almost pleased when London came under renewed assault from Hitler's new weapon – the V1 flying bomb. But it was a short-lived improvement. For much of July and August, talk turned once again to his dwindling ability to conduct the business of the war, and the pressure of another Allied Conference in Quebec in September seems to have made things worse.

Succour – and a revival of sorts – was to come with two further trips overseas. The first came in November when Churchill was able to visit Paris for the first time since it had been liberated in

August. It was a moment of enormous personal triumph and vindication – and a reminder of just how far he had come as leader since his frantic visits to the French capital in the weeks after he had succeeded Chamberlain. The second trip was in December, when Churchill made a dramatic intervention to try to bring a halt to the fighting that had broken out between rival military factions in Greece. Journeying to Athens on Christmas Day with the sound of gunfire uncomfortably close by, he attempted to broker a deal to establish a government acceptable to all.

It was a journey undertaken at great political as well as personal risk, with opposition parties accusing him of meddling in the democratic freedoms of a sovereign state. It was just the kind of controversial and dangerous adventure to stir Churchill's blood and – although the trip ended in failure – it is no coincidence that it was prefaced by a speech in the House of Commons of unusual power. It was a return to form for a Prime Minister who had recently celebrated his seventieth birthday, but how long would it last?

Previous page
Churchill observes the Allied landings in the South of France, August 1944.

Left
Churchill inspecting anti-flying bomb defences, in Southern England, 30 June 1944.

2 JANUARY

'They may say I lead them up the garden path, but at every stage of the garden they have found delectable fruit and wholesome vegetables.'

Churchill on his Chiefs of Staff, as recorded in a diary entry by his Private Secretary Jock Colville

Churchill and De Gaulle in Marrakesh, Morocco, on 13 January 1944.

7 JANUARY

'Winston, sitting in Marrakesh, is now full of beans and trying to win the war from there! As a result a 3-cornered flow of telegrams in all directions is gradually resulting in utter confusion! I wish to God that he would come home and get under control.'

Diary entry by Alan Brooke, Chief of the Imperial General Staff, and newly raised to the rank of Field Marshal

15 JANUARY

'The House cheered and rose, a courteous, spontaneous welcome... but curiously cold. Churchill is not loved in the House.'

Diary entry by Conservative MP Sir Henry Channon on Churchill's surprise return to Parliament after illness

2 FEBRUARY

'Why break the handle of the coffee pot at this stage and burn your fingers trying to hold it, why not wait till we get to Rome, and let it cool off.'

Churchill on American proposals to depose the King and Prime Minister of Italy

7 FEBRUARY

'In the station lavatory at Blackheath last week I found scrawled up, "Winston Churchill is a bastard." I pointed it out to the Wing Commander who was with me. "Yes," he said, "the tide has turned. We find it everywhere... the men hate politicians."'

Diary entry by Conservative MP Harold Nicolson

14 FEBRUARY

'I OFTEN DOUBT WHETHER I AM GOING MAD OR WHETHER HE IS REALLY SANE.'

Diary entry by Field Marshal Alan Brooke, Chief of the Imperial General Staff

Churchill talks with members of a US airborne unit and American war correspondents, March 1944.

22 FEBRUARY

'There are many dangers and difficulties in making speeches at this moment... There was a time when we were all alone in this war and when we could speak for ourselves, but now that we are in the closest relation on either side with our great Allies, every word spoken has to be considered in relation to them.'

Churchill in a speech to the House of Commons

'[He] told me it was a great effort to him to make these speeches now.'

Jock Colville, Churchill's Private Secretary, notes in his diary

29 FEBRUARY

'We hoped to land a wildcat that would tear out the bowels of the Boche. Instead we have stranded a vast whale with its tail flopping about in the water.'

Churchill on the Allied landings at Anzio in Italy, as recorded in the diary of Field Marshal Alan Brooke

Soldiers watch landing
operations at Anzio,
January 1944.

21 MARCH

'PM this morning confessed he was tired —
he's almost done in... Everyone's exhausted.'

Diary entry by Sir Alexander Cadogan, head of the Foreign Office

'HEAVEN KNOWS WHERE WE ARE GOING. I FEEL LIKE A MAN CHAINED TO THE CHARIOT OF A LUNATIC!!'

Diary entry by Field Marshal Alan Brooke, Chief of the Imperial General Staff

Churchill, using a Thompson 'Tommy' submachine gun, and General Dwight D Eisenhower take aim as American soldiers look on, March 1944.

26 MARCH

**'I hope you will not imagine that I am going to...
tell you exactly how all the problems of mankind
in war and peace are going to be solved...'**

*Churchill opening his first broadcast speech to the nation
in almost exactly a year*

'People seem to think that Winston's broadcast last
night was that of a worn and petulant old man. I am
sickened by the absence of gratitude towards him.
The fact is that the country is terribly war-weary...'

*Conservative MP Harold Nicolson discusses the reaction
to Churchill's speech in his diary*

2 APRIL

**'I am not going to tumble round my cage
like a wounded canary. You knocked me
off my perch. You have now got to put me
back on my perch. Otherwise I won't sing.'**

*Churchill privately explains to an MP why he will insist on
a vote of confidence, after his government's Education Bill
is voted down in Parliament*

19 APRIL

'PM, I fear, is breaking down.
He rambles without a pause...
I really don't know whether
he can carry on.'

Diary entry by Sir Alexander Cadogan,
head of the Foreign Office

Churchill on the veranda of
Navy House, Arromanches,
Normandy, July 1944.

20 APRIL

'I'D RUN LIKE HELL
TO HELP HITLER,
IF I WERE A HUN!'

Churchill remarking privately on the choice
facing the increasingly beleaguered Germans

25 APRIL

'What fun it would be to get there before Monty.'

Churchill on his desire to be among the first on the Normandy beachhead, as recorded in the diary of Jock Colville, his Private Secretary

26 APRIL

'Cyril Radcliffe [Director General of the Ministry of Information] thinks that there will be an anti-Tory landslide at the next Election & that even Victory & Winston will be powerless to save them.'

Diary entry by Churchill's friend, Violet Bonham Carter

7 MAY

'[Winston] said he could still always sleep well, eat well and especially drink well! but [*sic*] that he no longer jumped out of bed the way he used to, and felt as if he would be quite content to spend the whole day in bed. I have never yet heard him admit that he was beginning to fail.'

Diary entry by Field Marshal Alan Brooke,
Chief of the Imperial General Staff

Churchill and Eisenhower during their tour of troops preparing for D-Day near Lydd and Hastings in Kent, 12 May 1944.

13 MAY

'Whatever the PM's shortcomings may be, there is no doubt that he does provide guidance and purpose for the Chiefs of Staff and the [Foreign Office] on matters which, without him, would often be lost in the maze of inter-departmentalism or frittered away by caution and compromise. Moreover he has two qualities, imagination and resolution, which are conspicuously lacking among other Ministers and among the Chiefs of Staff. I hear him much criticised, often by people in close contact with him, but I think much of the criticism is due to the inability to see people and their actions in the right perspective when one examines them at quarters too close.'

Jock Colville, Churchill's Private Secretary, comments in his diary

4 JUNE

'Cross Channel operation... put off. Winston meanwhile... is touring the Portsmouth area and making a thorough pest of himself!'

Diary entry by Field Marshal Alan Brooke,
Chief of the Imperial General Staff

6 JUNE

'[WINSTON] LOOKED AS WHITE AS A SHEET... WE FEARED THAT HE WAS ABOUT TO ANNOUNCE SOME TERRIBLE DISASTER.'

Conservative MP Harold Nicolson describes the scene in the House of Commons as Churchill prepares to deliver what would prove to be a momentous statement

'I have also to announce to the House that during the night and the early hours of this morning THE FIRST OF THE SERIES OF LANDINGS IN FORCE UPON THE EUROPEAN CONTINENT HAS TAKEN PLACE. In this case the liberating assault fell upon the coast of France...

So far the Commanders who are engaged report that everything is proceeding according to plan. And what a plan! This vast operation is undoubtedly the most complicated and difficult that has ever taken place.'

Churchill announcing the Normandy landings to the House of Commons

Troops of 9th Canadian Infantry Brigade disembarking shortly before midday, 6 June 1944 (D-Day).

Churchill visits Montgomery (and his dog, Rommel) at his headquarters in Chateau Creully to receive first hand information on the Allied advance since D-Day, 7 August 1944.

8 JUNE

'I am sure that the mistakes of that time will not be repeated; we shall probably make another set of mistakes.'

Churchill in the House of Commons on the question of imposing war reparations on Germany

9 JUNE

'PM, who seems to have been baffled in his attempt to go to [the Normandy] Beaches, is mucking up foreign affairs instead.'

Diary entry by Sir Alexander Cadogan, head of the Foreign Office

19 JUNE

'Long Cabinet at which Winston was in very good form, quite 10 years younger, all due to the fact that the [German] flying bombs have again put us into the front line!!'

Field Marshal Alan Brooke, Chief of the Imperial General Staff, describes a change of Churchill's mood in his diary

Churchill on his visit to Caen, Normandy, 22 July 1944.

25 JUNE

'I AM AN OLD AND WEARY MAN. I FEEL EXHAUSTED.'

Churchill in conversation with his wife Clementine and Harold Macmillan, as recorded in the latter's diary

1 AUGUST

'When I was at Teheran [sic] I realised for the first time what a very small country this is. On one hand the big Russian bear with its paws outstretched – on the other the great American Elephant – and between them the poor little British donkey – who is the only one who knows the right way home.'

Churchill in a private remark on Britain's waning influence

2 AUGUST

'War is a hard school, but the British, once compelled to go there, are attentive pupils.'

Churchill in a speech to the House of Commons

Churchill watches an assault
against enemy positions north
of Florence on 20 August 1944.

3 AUGUST

'It's terrible that we have a PM who simply *can't conduct business*. It's all hot air!'

Diary entry by Sir Alexander Cadogan, head of the Foreign Office

5 AUGUST

'Everything seems to point to the speed-up of the war's ending... Anyway, if Churchill can bring himself to say so it's probably true: he isn't exactly prone to over-sanguine optimism, is he?'

British housewife Elizabeth Belsey in a letter to her serviceman husband

16 AUGUST

'He did not much enjoy his trip... he did not see enough shooting and fighting...'

Harold Macmillan, British Minister Resident in North Africa, writes in his diary about Churchill's journey to the South of France

10 SEPTEMBER

'[It] makes my blood boil to listen to his nonsense... And the wonderful thing is that ¾ of the population of the world imagine that Winston Churchill is one of the Strategists of History... It is far better that the world should never know, and never suspect the feet of clay of that otherwise superhuman being. Without him England was lost for a certainty, with him England has been on the verge of disaster time and again... NEVER HAVE I ADMIRED AND DESPISED A MAN SIMULTANEOUSLY TO THE SAME EXTENT.'

Diary entry by Field Marshal Alan Brooke, Chief of the Imperial General Staff, voyaging with Churchill to the Quebec Conference

28 SEPTEMBER

'When Herr Hitler escaped his bomb on July 20th he described his survival as providential; I think that from a purely military point of view we can all agree with him, for certainly it would be most unfortunate if the Allies were to be deprived, in the closing phases of the struggle, of that form of warlike genius... which Corporal Schickel-gruber has so notably contributed...'

Churchill mocks Hitler in a review of the war in the House of Commons

Churchill at Eighth Army Headquarters in Italy, 26 August 1944.

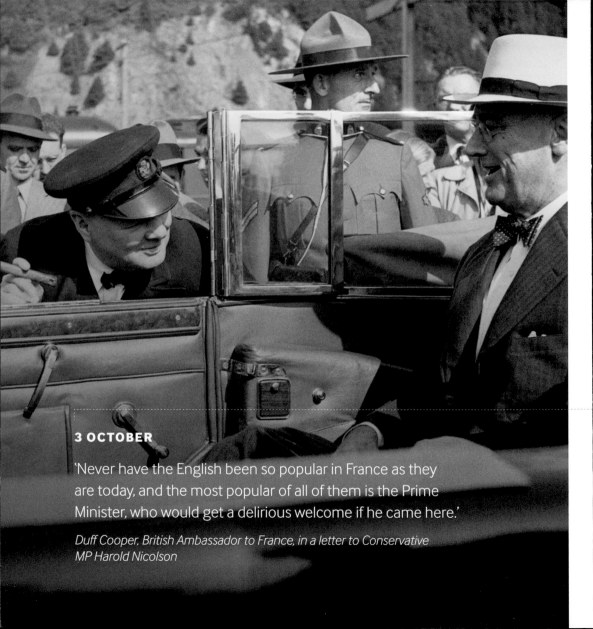

3 OCTOBER

'Never have the English been so popular in France as they are today, and the most popular of all of them is the Prime Minister, who would get a delirious welcome if he came here.'

Duff Cooper, British Ambassador to France, in a letter to Conservative MP Harold Nicolson

Churchill greets Roosevelt after arriving for the Quebec Conference in Canada, 11 September 1944.

27 OCTOBER

'We believe that we are in the last lap, but this is a race in which failure to exert the fullest effort to the end may postpone that end to periods almost unendurable.'

Churchill in a speech to the House of Commons

'"Collins", [Winston] said to the barman, "I should like a whisky-and-soda – single." He sat down in an armchair. He then struggled out of his armchair and walked again to the bar. "Collins", he said, "delete the word 'single' and insert the word 'double'." Then, grinning at us like a schoolboy, he resumed his seat.'

Conservative MP Harold Nicolson writes a letter to his sons describing an exchange in the House of Commons smoking room after Churchill's speech

31 OCTOBER

'A battle hangs like a curtain across the future. Once that curtain is raised or rent we can all see how the scenery is arranged, what actors are left upon the scene, and how they appear to be related to one another.'

Churchill in the chamber of the House of Commons, looking to the possibility of a General Election

12 NOVEMBER

'It is with the most vivid sensations that I find myself here this afternoon. I am going to give you a warning: be on your guard, because I am going to speak, or try to speak, in French, a formidable undertaking and one which will put great demands on your friendship for Great Britain.'

Churchill in a speech at the Hôtel de Ville in Paris

Churchill delivers a speech during a celebration of American Thanksgiving Day at the Royal Albert Hall in London, 23 November 1944.

'Don't know what it conveyed to the natives, but it was very forceful, and tearful, with a lot of table-thumping!'

Diary entry by Sir Alexander Cadogan, head of the Foreign Office, reacting to Churchill's speech in Paris

'Not for one moment did Winston stop crying... he could have filled buckets by the time he received the Freedom of Paris.'

Conservative MP Harold Nicolson describes the same trip in his diary

29 NOVEMBER

'I know the British people and I know this House, and there is one thing they will not stand, and that is not being told how bad things are...'

Churchill in a speech to Parliament

Winston Churchill and General
Charles de Gaulle at the
French armistice day parade
in Paris, 11 November 1944.

8 DECEMBER

'During the war... we have had to arm anyone who could shoot a Hun. Apart from their character, political convictions, past records and so forth, if they were out to shoot a Hun, we accepted them as friends and tried to enable them to fulfil their healthy instincts... But when countries are liberated, it does not follow that those who have received our weapons should use them in order to engross to themselves by violence and murder and bloodshed all those powers and traditions and continuity which many countries have slowly developed [...]

We did not feel it compatible with our honour [to] [...] leave Athens to anarchy and misery, followed by tyranny established on murder... If I am blamed for this action, I will gladly accept my dismissal at the hands of the House...'

Churchill speaking against a motion condemning the government's intervention in Greece

'A superb Parliamentary performance and its courage magnificent.'

Diary entry by Harold Macmillan, British Minister Resident in North Africa

'AS NO OTHER COULD HAVE DONE'

With military events taking on a momentum of their own, Churchill turns his thoughts towards post-war politics – at first with reluctance but then with electioneering zeal.

As the New Year dawned in 1945, German troops were fighting ferociously to reinvigorate the massive offensive that they had launched in the Ardennes just before Christmas. The Japanese were contesting every inch of an Allied advance back into Burma. And the remorseless Alpine winter had pinned down combatants on both sides in northern Italy. On the streets of London, as V2 rockets – the world's first ballistic missiles – rained down in ever greater numbers, the much predicted end to the war must have seemed like a distant prospect.

Churchill himself spent much of January locked away in the stygian depths of the Cabinet War Rooms, monitoring the progress of events and preparing for a second conference of the 'Big Three' – this time at Yalta on the shores of the Black Sea. It was a gloomy prospect for the Prime Minister. When he had first met with Roosevelt and Stalin in Tehran in November 1943, he had been struck by how dwarfed Britain was in comparison to its two superpower Allies. Now, as the post-war world loomed, he felt all the more frustrated and weighed down by the struggle to exert a telling influence.

After the conference, Churchill was only too pleased to get away, embarking on his last major journey of the war, stopping off in Athens, Alexandria and Cairo on his way back to London. There he seems to have experienced another dip in his health to the extent that he had to be carried up the stairs from the

Cabinet War Rooms after meetings. This evident infirmity perhaps made the news of Roosevelt's death in April all the harder to take. It is also striking how far removed Churchill seems to be during this period from the dramatic military progress being made – especially in the war against Germany. There is almost a sense that the war is continuing without him.

By the end of April another world leader had departed the stage – this time Adolf Hitler, who committed suicide in his Berlin bunker on the final day of the month. A telegram sent a few days later by Churchill to his wife Clementine reveals much about his attitude at this time. 'It is astonishing one is not in a more buoyant frame of mind,' he writes, explaining that 'beneath these triumphs lie poisonous politics and deadly international rivalries.'

Nonetheless, when Victory in Europe Day was declared for 8 May, it marked an enormous personal triumph for Churchill, and he played a central role in the celebrations. At Buckingham Palace, over the airwaves, at the House of Commons and, of course, in his travels through the streets of London, he was the lightning rod for the joy and thanksgiving that pulsed from every heart. His were the words that announced the victory, his the words that brought home its full significance. From the formality of his official radio address in the afternoon to the impromptu words delivered from a Whitehall balcony later that night, Churchill rose to the occasion. The voice of Britain's war had become the voice of its victory.

He was not, however, to be the voice of Britain's peace. The end of the war in Europe brought with it the break-up of Churchill's coalition government and the announcement of a General Election to be held on 5 July. The war against Japan may have been continuing but the Labour Party in particular was no longer prepared to work under Churchill's leadership. It was time to seek a fresh mandate from the British people.

Having professed a reluctance to return to the party political fray, Churchill fought the subsequent election campaign with great vigour and no little bile. He cut a divisive figure, deliberately provoking the opposition with his 'Vote National' slogan and suggesting that the Labour Party would introduce 'some kind of Gestapo'. Opinion was also divided on how his personal popularity would affect the outcome of the election, with speculation continuing throughout the three week period that followed the closing of the polls to allow votes to come in from the millions of troops abroad.

The announcement came on 26 July in the middle of the third conference of the 'Big Three' in Potsdam, just outside Berlin. Churchill had spent a week talking with Stalin and the new US President Harry Truman about the shape of the post-war world. He had also heard news about the successful US tests of the atomic bomb, and was quick to understand their significance for the short and longer-term future. But it was a future in which he would not play an immediate role. When he returned to London part way through the conference, it was to learn that he had lost in a landslide.

And so it was that when the atomic bomb was first dropped over Hiroshima barely a week later, and Japan was forced into surrender on 14 August, Churchill's was not the voice that made the announcements. His war of words was over.

Previous page
Churchill waves to crowds in Whitehall on the day he broadcast to the nation that the war with Germany had been won, 8 May 1945.

1 JANUARY

'The Nazi beast is cornered and… its destruction is inevitable.'

A New Year message from Churchill to resistance groups in Denmark

The 'Big Three', Winston Churchill, President Roosevelt and Marshal Stalin, sit for a group photograph outside the Livadia Palace during the Yalta Conference, February 1945.

18 JANUARY

'Can we produce that complete unity and that new impulse in time to achieve decisive military victory with the least possible prolongation of the world's misery, or must we fall into jabber, babel [*sic*] and discord while victory is still unattained? … Very often have the triumphs and sacrifices of armies come to naught at the conference table. Very often the eagles have been squalled down by the parrots…'

Churchill opening a debate on the war situation in the House of Commons

'Witty and combative… the best effort I have heard him make since 1941 or even 1940.'

Jock Colville, Churchill's Private Secretary, reacts to the speech in his diary

'These are great days. These are days when dawn is bright, when darkness rolls away. A great future lies before your great country.'

Churchill addressing a crowd in Athens

20 FEBRUARY

'Accompanied the PM to the House for Questions. He was received with cheers.'

Diary entry by Jock Colville, Churchill's Private Secretary on the Prime Minister's return from the Yalta Conference

22 FEBRUARY

'How have we conducted this war, with the PM spending hours of his own and other people's time simply drivelling, welcoming every red herring so as only to have the pleasure of more irrelevant, redundant talk?'

Diary entry by Sir Alexander Cadogan, head of the Foreign Office

27 FEBRUARY

'I must admit that in all this war I never felt so grave a responsibility as I did at Yalta. In 1940 and 1941, when... invasion was so near, the actual steps one ought to take and our attitude towards them seemed plain and simple. If a man is coming across the sea to kill you, you do everything in your power to make sure he dies before finishing his journey. That may be difficult, it may be painful, but at least it is simple. Now we are entering a world of imponderables, and at every stage occasions for self-questioning arise.'

Churchill comparing the challenges of 1940 and 1945 in a speech on the war situation in the House of Commons

Churchill and Stalin pictured during a break in the Yalta Conference, February 1945.

⌄

'[Winston] seemed in wonderful form during his speech, but he confessed afterwards that he felt "tired all through".'

Conservative MP Harold Nicolson notes in his diary

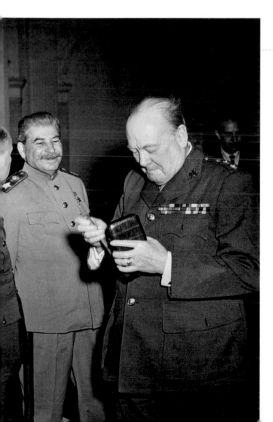

7 MARCH

'He will run a very grave risk of falling into senility before he is over-taken by old age.'

Churchill rebuking a fellow MP on his ignorance of House of Commons procedure

15 MARCH

'You hear all this talk by the stay-at-home Left Wing [*sic*] intelligentsia that the soldiers will hold us guilty if we do not have a new world waiting for them on their return... But that is not what the fighting men are looking forward to... When they are home and settled down, when our country is again a going concern, paying its way and standing on its own feet in the post-war world, then it will be the time for them to settle what form and shape our society should assume.'

Churchill speaking to the Conservative party about a potential General Election

'A good fighting speech which ought to win the next election.'

Conservative MP Sir Henry Channon reacts to the speech in his diary

'After the Cabinet, which is held in the [Cabinet War Room] nowadays because of V2s, the PM sits in a chair and is carried upstairs backwards by three stalwart marines. The Cabinet trail behind and the general effect of the procession is utterly ludicrous.'

Diary entry by Jock Colville, Churchill's Private Secretary

Posters looking to the future such as the above by Maurice A Brownfoot became more commonplace as Allied victory seemed assured.

20 MARCH

'The PM is losing interest in the war, because he no longer has control of military affairs. Up till [the Normandy landings] he saw himself as... the supreme authority to whom all military decisions were referred. Now, in all but questions of wide- and long-term strategy, he is by force of circumstances little more than a spectator. Thus he turns his energies to politics and the coming General Election.'

A remark by Leslie Rowan, one of Churchill's Private Secretaries, as recorded in the diary of his colleague Jock Colville

Churchill on the east bank of the Rhine, south of Wesel, 25 March 1945.

Churchill and Roosevelt confer during a lunch break at the Yalta Conference, February 1945.

13 APRIL

'Awful news about [the death of] Roosevelt. I feel deeply for Winston... it was evident from his manner that it was a real body blow.'

Conservative MP Harold Nicolson in a letter to his wife

17 APRIL

**'The greatest American friend
we have ever known, and the
greatest champion of freedom
who has ever brought help
and comfort from the new
world to the old.'**

*Churchill paying tribute to President
Roosevelt in the House of Commons*

19 APRIL

**'No words can express the horror which is felt
by His Majesty's Government and their principal
Allies at the proofs of these frightful crimes
now daily coming into view.'**

*Churchill on reports coming through from newly liberated
concentration camps, including Bergen-Belsen which was
reached by Allied troops four days earlier*

26 APRIL

'[The PM's] vanity was astonishing and I am glad [Stalin] does not know what effect a few kind words, after so many harsh ones, might well have on our policy towards Russia.'

Jock Colville, Churchill's Private Secretary, writes in his diary about the Prime Minister's reaction to a friendly telegram from Stalin

1 MAY

'The PM can be counted on to score a hundred in a Test Match but is no good at village cricket.'

A remark by General Hastings Ismay, Churchill's Chief of Staff, as recorded in the diary of Jock Colville

Churchill seated at his desk in the No 10 Annexe Map Room, May 1945.

4 MAY

'[The PM] was evidently seriously affected by the fact that the war was to all intents and purposes over as far as Germany was concerned. HE THANKED US ALL VERY NICELY AND WITH TEARS IN HIS EYES FOR ALL WE HAD DONE IN THE WAR, AND ALL THE ENDLESS WORK WE HAD PUT IN "FROM EL ALAMEIN TO WHERE WE ARE NOW". HE THEN SHOOK HANDS WITH ALL OF US.'

Diary entry by Field Marshal Alan Brooke, Chief of the Imperial General Staff

5 MAY

'It is astonishing one is not in a more buoyant frame of mind in public matters. During the last three days we have heard of the death of Mussolini and Hitler; Alexander has taken a million prisoners of war... All north-west Germany, Holland and Denmark are to be surrendered early tomorrow morning with all troops and ships etc... Meanwhile I need scarcely tell you that beneath these triumphs lie poisonous politics and deadly international rivalries.'

Churchill in a telegram to Clementine, who was away on a trip to Moscow

8 MAY

'Yesterday morning at 2.41am at Headquarters, General Jodl, the representative of the German High Command, and Grand Admiral Doenitz, the designated head of the German State, signed the act of unconditional surrender of all German land, sea and air forces in Europe... The German war is therefore at an end... We may allow ourselves a brief period of rejoicing; but let us not forget for a moment the toil and efforts that lie ahead. Japan, with all her treachery and greed, remains unsubdued.'

Churchill announcing the unconditional surrender of Germany

'As Big Ben struck three, there was an extraordinary hush over the assembled multitude, and then came Winston's voice. He was short and effective... "The evil-doers," he intoned, "now lie prostrate before us." The crowd gasped at this phrase. "Advance Britannia!" he shouted at the end... and then cheer upon cheer.'

Conservative MP Harold Nicolson describes the scene outside Parliament in a letter to his son

'Winston, smiling and bent, appeared and had a great reception. Everyone... rose and cheered and waved handkerchiefs and Order Papers... but his reception, even at a supreme moment like today, did not equal Mr Chamberlain's great ovation after Munich.'

Diary entry by Conservative MP Sir Henry Channon

Churchill makes his VE Day broadcast to the British public, announcing that the war with Germany is over, 3pm, 8 May 1945.

HM King George VI and Queen Elizabeth with Princess Elizabeth and Princess Margaret are joined by Winston Churchill on the balcony of Buckingham Palace, London on VE Day, 8 May 1945.

'Beloved Winston... On this day of days the love & immeasurable thankfulness of the whole nation goes out to you. You have led, inspired and sustained us *as no other could have done.* This war began long before 1939. You were leading us then – & I am proud to have been with you from the start to this our Journey's End.'

Violet Bonham Carter in a letter to her friend Churchill

'GOD BLESS YOU ALL. THIS IS YOUR VICTORY! It is the victory of the cause of freedom in every land. In all our long history we have never seen a greater day than this. Everyone, man or woman, has done their best. Everyone has tried. Neither the long years, nor the dangers, nor the fierce attacks of the enemy, have in any way weakened the independent resolve of the British nation. God bless you all.'

Churchill speaks to the crowds from the balcony of the Ministry of Health

'We ran like mad to see what was happening and arrived just as the Prime Minister had appeared on the balcony! ... Everyone shouted of course and at last Mr Churchill made us a speech which I'm sure was impromptu... He was thanking London for their courage, but nobody wanted to be serious, and he knew just the right jokes to make... He had terrific applause, doubled when he waved his hat and puffed his cigar — which he did deliberately.'

A young British woman, Miss F E Tate, writes to her mother describing being among the crowds on VE Day

'ALL MY THOUGHTS ARE WITH YOU ON THIS DAY WHICH IS SO ESSENTIALLY YOUR DAY. IT IS YOU WHO HAVE LED, UPLIFTED AND INSPIRED US THROUGH THE WORST DAYS. WITHOUT YOU THIS DAY COULD NOT HAVE BEEN.'

A telegram to Churchill sent by Foreign Secretary Anthony Eden

VE Day celebrations
in London, 8 May 1945.

'Nearly six years since those early days of September 1939 – and Churchill has seen it through. CHURCHILL!! WHAT A MAN! WE OWE MORE TO HIM THAN WE KNOW. When the future looked black Churchill put a shine on it. It was still black but it was a brilliant black not a dead black. When things looked bright Churchill drew attention to the dark clouds which still threatened. He kept us on an even keel, with the engine even running at full speed. Now what!'

Diary entry by local government officer Mr W A Rodgers

11 MAY

'It was a bitter thought that, having been a national leader for so long, and having been so kindly treated by all, he would soon be attacked and spoken ill of by nearly half the nation.'

Diary entry by Labour MP and government minister Hugh Dalton reporting a remark made by Churchill to a colleague

13 MAY

'I wish I could tell you tonight that all our toils and troubles were over. Then indeed I could end my five years' service happily, and if you thought that you had had enough of me and that I ought to be put out to grass, I tell you that I would take it with the best of grace...

I told you hard things at the beginning of these last five years; you did not shrink, and I should be unworthy of your confidence and generosity if I still did not cry: Forward, unflinching, unswerving, indomitable, till the whole task is done and the whole world is safe and clean.'

Churchill in a broadcast to the world

'In a way the most moving I have ever heard him make.'

Diary entry by Churchill's friend and noted liberal Violet Bonham Carter

VE Day celebrations, 8 May 1945.

17 MAY

'The PM tells me he feels overpowered by the prospect of a meeting with the "Big Three"... weighed down by the responsibility and the uncertainty.'

Diary entry by Jock Colville, Churchill's Private Secretary

Churchill, Truman and Stalin at the Potsdam Conference, 23 July 1945.

Churchill and US President Harry Truman shake hands on the steps of Truman's residence in Babelsberg, Germany, on 16 July 1945.

19 MAY

'It takes rather a long time now to talk with the PM. He thinks and talks of so many things at once. But I find that if one ploughs steadily on, what one says sinks in.'

Diary entry by Harold Macmillan, British Minister Resident in North Africa

27 MAY

'People feel, in a vague and muddled way, that all the sacrifices to which they have been exposed and their separation... from family life during four or five years, are all the fault of "them" — namely the authority or the Government. By a totally illogical process of reasoning, they believe that "they" mean the upper classes, or the Conservatives, and that in some manner... all that went ill was due to Churchill.'

Conservative MP Harold Nicolson discusses the forthcoming election in a letter to his son

28 MAY

'Standing behind the Cabinet table... [Churchill] addressed us all, with tears visibly running down his cheeks. He said that we had all come together, and had stayed together as a united band of friends, in a very trying time. History would recognise this. "The light will shine on every helmet."'

Diary entry by Labour MP and government minister Hugh Dalton on the break-up of the coalition government

4 JUNE

'No Socialist Government conducting the entire life and industry of the country could afford to allow free, sharp, or violently-worded expressions of public discontent. They would have to fall back on some form of Gestapo... I stand for the sovereign freedom of the individual... I stand for the rights of the ordinary man to say what he thinks of the Government...'

Churchill in his first election broadcast

'[He] really does lay it on a bit thick!'

Diary entry by Churchill's friend Violet Bonham Carter

Churchill during the election campaign, 27 June 1945.

10 JUNE

'The war lords are temperamentally incapable of conducting peace. Thank goodness, Roosevelt is gone and we have Mr Truman, the plain American citizen, honest, forthright, we all want Truman now! But Winston... has now launched out on a jingo election which is terrifying in its inappropriateness. He will have the whole country at war with itself soon.'

Foreign Office official Oliver Harvey in his diary

20 JUNE

'He is very low, poor Darling. He thinks he has lost his "touch" & he grieves about it.'

Clementine Churchill in a letter to her daughter Mary

22 JUNE

'You know I have an admiration for Winston amounting to idolatry, so I am dreadfully distressed by the badness of his broadcast Election speeches. WHAT HAS GONE WRONG WITH HIM? They are confused, woolly, unconstructive and so wordy that it is impossible to pick out any concrete impression from them.'

Vita Sackville-West in a letter to her husband, Conservative MP Harold Nicolson

10 JULY

'I don't think [Churchill] is any longer needed for the war. I think him quite the wrong man for directing the reconstruction of England. OUR DEBT TO HIM IS PROBABLY GREATER THAN TO ANY OTHER POLITICIAN IN OUR HISTORY, BUT I COULD NOT FEEL ON THAT ACCOUNT ANY OBLIGATION TO VOTE FOR HIM.'

Writer Raymond Mortimer in a letter to Conservative MP Harold Nicolson

< Churchill sits on one of
the damaged chairs from
Hitler's bunker in Berlin,
16 July 1945.

23 JULY

'[The PM] had seen the reports of the American... secret explosive experiments [the atomic bomb]... and was completely carried away! It was now no longer necessary for the Russians to come into the Japanese war, the new explosive alone was sufficient to settle the matter. Furthermore we now had something in our hands which would redress the balance with the Russians! The secret of this explosive, and the power to use it, would completely alter the diplomatic equilibrium which was adrift since the defeat of Germany! ... Now we could say if you insist on doing this or that, well we can just blot out Moscow, then Stalingrad, then Kiev... And now where are the Russians!!!'

Diary entry by Field Marshal Alan Brooke, Chief of the Imperial General Staff, disparaging Churchill's perceptive reaction to the successful testing of the atomic bomb

'CHURCHILL IS OUT AND ATTLEE HAS A CLEAR MAJORITY! NOBODY FORESAW THIS AT ALL.'

Conservative MP Harold Nicolson in his diary

'A terrible blow to poor old Winston, and I am awfully sorry for the old boy. It certainly is a display of base ingratitude, and rather humiliating for our country.'

Diary entry by Sir Alexander Cadogan, head of the Foreign Office

'The decision of the British people has been recorded... I have therefore laid down the charge which was placed upon me in darker times. I regret that I have not been permitted to finish the work against Japan... It only remains for me to express to the British people, for whom I have acted in these perilous years, my profound gratitude for the unflinching, unswerving support which they have given me during my task, and for the many expressions of kindness which they have shown towards their servant.'

A statement issued by Churchill after the declaration of the General Election result

King George VI stands with the new Labour Prime Minister, Clement Attlee, in the grounds of Buckingham Palace, 26 July 1945.

27 JULY

'A DAY OF PARTINGS! ... IT WAS A VERY SAD AND MOVING LITTLE MEETING AT WHICH I FOUND MYSELF UNABLE TO SAY MUCH FOR FEAR OF BREAKING DOWN. [WINSTON] WAS STANDING THE BLOW WONDERFULLY WELL.'

Field Marshal Alan Brooke, Chief of the Imperial General Staff reflects in his diary

29 JULY

'FINIS'

Churchill's entry in the visitors' book at Chequers, where he was allowed to enjoy one final weekend

14 AUGUST

'[We] listened together & heard the Japanese surrender announced by Attlee. One thought "*how* hard for Winston! & how differently he wld [*sic*] have done it"'

Churchill's friend Violet Bonham Carter in her diary

15 AUGUST

'I drove to the House with Mr Attlee through exuberant crowds. Winston received the greatest ovation of all.'

Jock Colville, now Private Secretary to Prime Minister Attlee, makes a diary entry describing Victory over Japan Day

16 AUGUST

'The morrow of such a victory as we have gained is a splendid moment both in our small lives and in our great history. It is a time not only of rejoicing but even more of resolve. When we look back on all the perils through which we have passed and at the mighty foes we have laid low and all the dark and deadly designs we have frustrated, why should we fear for our future? We have come safely through the worst.

"Home is the sailor, home from sea, And the hunter home from the hill."'

Churchill concludes his first major speech in the House of Commons as Leader of the Opposition

SOURCES

1939

Admiralty Papers, The National Archives, 116/4239

Amery Papers, Churchill Archives Centre,
Cambridge University

Baruch Papers, Princeton University Library

Cabinet Papers, The National Archives, 66/4

Churchill Papers 2/365, Churchill Papers 8/629,
Churchill Papers 9/138, reproduced with permission
of Curtis Brown, London on behalf of The Estate
of Winston S. Churchill, © The Estate of
Winston S. Churchill

Churchill, Winston S: *Into Battle* (1941) reproduced
with permission of Curtis Brown, London on
behalf of The Estate of Winston S. Churchill,
© The Estate of Winston S. Churchill

Colville, John: *The Fringes of Power: Downing Street
Diaries* 1939-55 (1985)

Dilks, David (ed.): *The Diaries of Sir Alexander Cadogan,
1938-1945* (1971)

Foreign Office Papers, The National Archives,
FO 371/22974

Gilbert, Martin: *Winston S. Churchill, Vol. 5,
Prophet of Truth 1922-39* (2009)

HC Debate 13 April 1939, 2 August 1939,
3 September 1939

Macleod, Colonel Roderick & Kelly, Denis (eds):
The Ironside Diaries: 1937-1940 (1962)

Nicolson, Nigel (ed): *Harold Nicolson: Diaries and
Letters,1939-45* (1966) © The Estate of
Sir Harold Nicolson

Rhodes-James, Robert (ed.): *'Chips': The Diaries of
Sir Henry Channon* (1967)

Soames, Mary (ed.): Speaking for Themselves:
*The Personal Letters of Winston and Clementine
Churchill* (1999)

Templewood Papers, Cambridge University Library

The papers of John Allsebrook Simon, 1st Viscount
Simon, Bodleian Library

1940

Baroness Spencer-Churchill Papers, reproduced with
permission of Curtis Brown, London on behalf of
the Master, Fellows and Scholars of Churchill College,
Cambridge, © Master, Fellows and Scholars of
Churchill College, Cambridge

Churchill, Winston S: *Into Battle* (1941), reproduced
with permission of Curtis Brown, London on behalf
of The Estate of Winston S. Churchill, © The Estate
of Winston S. Churchill

Ciano, Galeazzo: *The War Diaries of Count Galeazzo
Ciano, 1939-43* (2015)

Colville, John: *The Fringes of Power: Downing Street
Diaries 1939-55* (1985)

Danchev, Alex and Todman, Daniel (eds.): *War Diaries
1939-45 Field Marshal Lord Alanbrooke* (1992)
© The Estate of Field Marshal Alan Francis Brooke,
1st Viscount Alanbrooke

Dilks, David (ed.): *The Diaries of Sir Alexander Cadogan,
1938-1945* (1971)

Gilbert, Martin: *Churchill: A Life* (1991), reproduced
with permission of Curtis Brown, London on behalf
of The Estate of Winston S. Churchill, © The Estate
of Winston S. Churchill

Gilbert: Martin: *Winston S. Churchill, Vol. 6, Finest Hour
1939-41* (2011)

Halifax Papers, Borthwick Institute, University of York

HC Debate 8 May 1940, 13 May 1940, 4 June 1940, 18 June 1940, 20 August 1940, 8 October 1940, 21 November 1940

Ickes Papers, Library of Congress

IWM Documents.11591

IWM Documents.16277

Martin, Sir John: *Downing Street: The War Years – Diaries, Letters and a Memoir* (1991)

Nicolson, Nigel (ed): Harold Nicolson: *Diaries and Letters, 1939-45* (1966) © The Estate of Sir Harold Nicolson

Pimlott, Ben (ed.): *The Second World War Diary of Hugh Dalton, 1940-45* (1986)

Pottle, Mark (ed.): *Champion Redoubtable: The Diaries and Letters of Violet Bonham Carter, 1914-45* (1998)

Quoted in Colville, John: *The Fringes of Power: Downing Street Diaries 1939-55* (1985), reproduced with permission of Curtis Brown, London on behalf of The Estate of Winston S. Churchill, © The Estate of Winston S. Churchill

Rhodes-James, Robert (ed.): *'Chips': The Diaries of Sir Henry Channon* (1967)

Second Earl of Birkenhead: *Halifax: The Life of Lord Halifax* (1965)

Taylor, Fred (ed.): *The Goebbels Diaries, 1939-41* (1982)

1941

Churchill, Winston S: *The Unrelenting Struggle* (1942), reproduced with permission of Curtis Brown, London on behalf of The Estate of Winston S. Churchill, © The Estate of Winston S. Churchill

Colville, John: *The Fringes of Power: Downing Street Diaries 1939-55* (1985)

Danchev, Alex and Todman, Daniel (eds.): *War Diaries 1939-45 Field Marshal Lord Alanbrooke* (1992) © The Estate of Field Marshal Alan Francis Brooke, 1st Viscount Alanbrooke

Harvey, John (ed.): *The War Diaries of Oliver Harvey* (1978), © The Estate of Sir Anthony Eden

HC Debate 7 May 1941, 10 June 1941, 9 September 1941, 30 September 1941, 12 November 1941, 8 December 1941, 11 December 1941

Nicolson, Nigel (ed): Harold Nicolson: *Diaries and Letters, 1939-45* (1966) © The Estate of Sir Harold Nicolson

Pimlott, Ben (ed.): *The Second World War Diary of Hugh Dalton, 1940-45* (1986)

Quoted in Colville, John: *The Fringes of Power: Downing Street Diaries 1939-55* (1985), reproduced with permission of Curtis Brown, London on behalf of The Estate of Winston S. Churchill, © The Estate of Winston S. Churchill

Rhodes-James, Robert (ed.): *'Chips': The Diaries of Sir Henry Channon* (1967)

Sherwood, Robert E. (ed.): *The White House Papers of Harry L Hopkins* (1949)

Taylor, Fred (ed.): *The Goebbels Diaries, 1939-41* (1982)

1942

© Mrs Elizabeth Belsey [IWM Documents.1766]

© FE Brown [IWM Documents.12472]

Churchill, Winston S: *The End of the Beginning* (1943), reproduced with permission of Curtis Brown, London on behalf of The Estate of Winston S. Churchill, © The Estate of Winston S. Churchill

Ciano, Galeazzo: *The War Diaries of Count Galeazzo Ciano, 1939-43* (2015)

Danchev, Alex and Todman, Daniel (eds.): *War Diaries 1939-45 Field Marshal Lord Alanbrooke* (1992) © The Estate of Field Marshal Alan Francis Brooke, 1st Viscount Alanbrooke

Dilks, David (ed.): *The Diaries of Sir Alexander Cadogan, 1938-1945* (1971)

© Michael James Gould [IWM Documents.12542]

Harvey, John (ed.): *The War Diaries of Oliver Harvey* (1978)

HC Debate 27 January 1942, 24 February 1942, 1 July 1942, 2 July 1942, 8 September 1942

Nicolson, Nigel (ed): *Harold Nicolson: Diaries and Letters, 1939-45* (1966) © The Estate of Sir Harold Nicolson

Pottle, Mark (ed.): *Champion Redoubtable: The Diaries and Letters of Violet Bonham Carter, 1914-45* (1998)

Rhodes-James, Robert (ed.): *'Chips': The Diaries of Sir Henry Channon* (1967)

© William Rodgers [IWM Documents 14912]

Soames, Mary (ed.): *Speaking for Themselves: The Personal Letters of Winston and Clementine Churchill* (1999)

1943

Churchill, Winston S: *Onwards to Victory* (1944), reproduced with permission of Curtis Brown, London on behalf of The Estate of Winston S. Churchill, © The Estate of Winston S. Churchill

Danchev, Alex and Todman, Daniel (eds.): *War Diaries 1939-45 Field Marshal Lord Alanbrooke* (1992) © The Estate of Field Marshal Alan Francis Brooke, 1st Viscount Alanbrooke

Dilks, David (ed.): *The Diaries of Sir Alexander Cadogan, 1938-1945* (1971)

© Sir Charles Gairdner [IWM Documents.12979]

Harvey, John (ed.): *The War Diaries of Oliver Harvey* (1978)

HC Debate 11 February 1943, 23 March 1943, 8 June 1943, 27 July 1943, 21 September 1943, 22 September 1943, 13 October 1943

Macmillan, Harold: *War Diaries: Politics and War in the Mediterranean, January 1943 – May 1945* (1985)

Martin, Sir John: *Downing Street: The War Years – Diaries, Letters and a Memoir* (1991)

Nicolson, Nigel (ed): *Harold Nicolson: Diaries and Letters, 1939-45* (1966) © The Estate of Sir Harold Nicolson

Pimlott, Ben (ed.): *The Second World War Diary of Hugh Dalton, 1940-45* (1986)

© EA Pye [IWM Documents.15215]

Rhodes-James, Robert (ed.): *'Chips': The Diaries of Sir Henry Channon* (1967)

Soames, Mary (ed.): *Speaking for Themselves: The Personal Letters of Winston and Clementine Churchill* (1999)

1944

© Mrs Elizabeth Belsey [IWM Documents.1766]

Churchill, Winston S: *The Dawn of Liberation* (1945), reproduced with permission of Curtis Brown, London on behalf of The Estate of Winston S. Churchill, © The Estate of Winston S. Churchill

Colville, John: *The Fringes of Power: Downing Street Diaries 1939-55* (1985)

Danchev, Alex and Todman, Daniel (eds.): *War Diaries 1939-45 Field Marshal Lord Alanbrooke* (1992) © The Estate of Field Marshal Alan Francis Brooke, 1st Viscount Alanbrooke

Dilks, David (ed.): *The Diaries of Sir Alexander Cadogan, 1938-1945* (1971)

HC Debate 22 February 1944, 6 June 1944,
   8 June 1944, 2 August 1944, 28 September 1944,
   27 October 1944, 31 October 1944,
   29 November 1944, 8 December 1944
Macmillan, Harold: *War Diaries: Politics and War in the
   Mediterranean, January 1943 – May 1945* (1985)
Nicolson, Nigel (ed): *Harold Nicolson: Diaries and
   Letters, 1939-45* (1966) © The Estate of
   Sir Harold Nicolson
Pottle, Mark (ed.): *Champion Redoubtable: The Diaries
   and Letters of Violet Bonham Carter, 1914-45* (1998)
Rhodes-James, Robert (ed.): *'Chips': The Diaries of
   Sir Henry Channon* (1967)

1945

Churchill, Winston S: *Onwards to Victory* (1944),
   reproduced with permission of Curtis Brown,
   London on behalf of The Estate of Winston S.
   Churchill, © The Estate of Winston S. Churchill
Colville, John: *The Fringes of Power: Downing Street
   Diaries 1939-55* (1985)
Danchev, Alex and Todman, Daniel (eds.): *War Diaries
   1939-45 Field Marshal Lord Alanbrooke* (1992)
   © The Estate of Field Marshal Alan Francis Brooke,
   1st Viscount Alanbrooke
Dilks, David (ed.): *The Diaries of Sir Alexander Cadogan,
   1938-1945* (1971)
© Sir Anthony Eden, Churchill Papers 20/218
Harvey, John (ed.): *The War Diaries of Oliver Harvey* (1978)
HC Debate 18 January 1945, 27 February 1945,
   7 March 1945, 17 April 1945, 19 April 1945,
   16 August 1945
Macmillan, Harold: *War Diaries: Politics and War in the
   Mediterranean, January 1943 – May 1945* (1985)

Nicolson, Nigel (ed): *Harold Nicolson: Diaries and
   Letters, 1939-45* (1966) © The Estate of Sir
   Harold Nicolson
Pimlott, Ben (ed.): *The Second World War Diary of
   Hugh Dalton, 1940-45* (1986)
Pottle, Mark (ed.): *Champion Redoubtable: The Diaries
   and Letters of Violet Bonham Carter, 1914-45* (1998)
Soames, Mary: *Clementine Churchill* (1982),
   reproduced with permission of Curtis Brown,
   London on behalf of The Estate of Winston S.
   Churchill, © The Estate of Winston S. Churchill
Rhodes-James, Robert (ed.): *'Chips': The Diaries of
   Sir Henry Channon* (1967)
© William Rodgers, Lord Rodgers of Quarry Bank
   [IWM Documents. 14912]
Letter from Vita Sackville West to Harold, 22nd
   July 1945 © The Estate of Vita Sackville West, 2011 /
Soames, Mary: *Clementine Churchill* (1982)
   reproduced with permission of Curtis Brown,
   London on behalf of The Estate of Winston S.
   Churchill, © The Estate of Winston S. Churchill
© FE Tate, [IWM Documents.3096]

SECONDARY SOURCES
Gilbert, Martin: *Churchill: A Life* (1991)
Gilbert: Martin: *Winston S. Churchill, Vol. 5,
   Prophet of Truth 1922–39* (2009)
Gilbert: Martin: *Winston S. Churchill, Vol. 6,
   Finest Hour 1939–41* (2011)
Gilbert: Martin: *Winston S. Churchill, Vol. 7,
   Road to Victory 1941–45* (2013)
Jenkins, Roy: *Churchill* (2002)
Meacham, Jon: *Franklin and Winston:
   A Portrait of a Friendship* (2004)

IMAGE LIST

All images © IWM unless otherwise stated. Every effort has been made to contact all copyright holders. The publishers will be glad to make good in future editions any error or omission brought to their attention.

Introduction: HU 90973. **1939:** HU 54737, HU 48566, HU 5547, D 2239, MH 13116, HU 45348, HU 100438, HU 5538, O 190, HU 51009, HU 51008, HU 86147, A 3.**1940:** MH 26392, PST 14971, HU 83283, HU 73115, H 2646A, HU 58256, NYP 45063, NYP 68075, HU 104755, CH 740, H 4366, HU 54420, H 2628, PST 8774, H 3508, H 3499, H 4985, H 3978, HU 91052, HU 36220).**1941:** A 4816, H 9155, H 6550, A 2736, PST 14228, H 9265, H 9157, H 11842, HU 111387, H 10688, H 10300, A 4825, H 15384, H 14266, HU 56120, NYP 54898, CAN 578.**1942:** H 16645, A 6920, A 11592, H 19765, MOI FLM 1115, HU 73755, H 20446, ME RAF 5060, E 15347, E 15905, TR 210, A 12648, H 25966, PST 2802.**1943:** K 5870, A 19210, NA 481, K 4473, A 17037, A 16753, A 17087, A 17604, A 17918, NA 3255, NA 3252, H 40334, H 32728, A 20723, A 20589, E 26640, NA 10074.**1944:** A 25248, H 39498, HU 60057, EA 18274, NA 11387, H 36960, A 24829, H 38458, A 23938, B 8766, TR 2047, NA 17912, TR 2272, H 40057, EA 44805, BU 1292.**1945:** H 41849, NAM 234, EA 52860, PST 14648, EA 52857, BU 2250, COL 30, H 41841, MH 21835, EA 65799, HU 41808, BU 9195, BU 8944, HU 55965, BU 8961, HU 59486, EPH 1406.

ACKNOWLEDGEMENTS

I would like to thank the publishing team at IWM for their help in bringing this book to completion. In particular I owe a significant debt to Julie McMahon, who delved so thoroughly into IWM's archives to unearth extracts from previously unpublished diaries and letters; to Ian Kikuchi for pointing out factual errors and infelicities in the text; to Georgia Davies for arriving at a design that so effectively brings the chronology and power of the selected quotes to life; and to Madeleine James for guiding me with such consideration towards making that final selection.

Of course the book would be nothing without the many contributing diarists and letter writers whose works are listed under Sources. It was a privilege to spend so much time in their company. I only wish I could have included more of their many remarkable insights, experiences and turns of phrase. I am also uncomfortably aware of the many sources that I have not mined. I hope readers will forgive me for any significant omissions.

Finally, I should pay tribute to Churchill himself. He was a man who understood the power of words, and who harnessed that power to extraordinary effect. I hope to have conveyed something of his genius in these pages, and to have offered readers a fresh, nuanced and candid appraisal of his personality, his qualities and his singular contribution to the winning of the Second World War.